Defending Against Biothreats:
What We Can Learn from the Coronavirus
Pandemic to Enhance U.S. Defenses Against
Pandemics and Biological Weapons

DEFENDING AGAINST BIOTHREATS

WHAT WE CAN LEARN
FROM THE
CORONAVIRUS PANDEMIC TO ENHANCE U.S. DEFENSES AGAINST PANDEMICS AND BIOLOGICAL WEAPONS

Fred Fleitz, Editor
Ken Alibek
Shoshana Bryen
Stephen Bryen
Gordon Chang
Paula DeSutter
Stephen Elliott
Charles Faddis
Jim Geraghty
Rosemary Gibson
John Lauder
Claudia Rosett
Albina Tskhay

ISBN-9798664380446

Defending Against Biothreats:
What We Can Learn from the Coronavirus Pandemic to Enhance
Our Defenses Against Pandemics and Biological Weapons
is published in the United States by the Center for Security
Policy Press, a division of the Center for Security Policy

July 23, 2020

THE CENTER FOR SECURITY POLICY
Washington, DC 20006
Phone: (202) 835-9077 | Email: info@securefreedom.org
For more information, please see securefreedom.org

Book Design by Bravura Books
Cover art by Oleg Atbashian

CONTENTS

Introduction.. 1
By Fred Fleitz

1. The Trail Leading Back to the Wuhan Labs............................ 9
By Jim Geraghty

2. China: The Cover-Up of the Greatest Crime of the
Century 23
By Gordon G. Chang

3. Lessons From the Coronavirus: Decouple From China to
Strengthen Biowarfare Preparedness 35
By Rosemary Gibson

4. A Chinese Communist Virus at the World Health
Organization...47
By Claudia Rosett

5. The Lessons Terrorists Will Draw from the Coronavirus
Pandemic 61
By Charles Faddis

6. Future Biowar: What the Bad Guys Have Learned and
How to Combat It..73
By Shoshana Bryen and Stephen Bryen

7. Understanding the Bioweapons Threat and Its
Implications for Defense Against Natural Epidemics...........83
By Ken Alibek and Albina Tskhay

8. How Can We Develop Reliable Defense in an Uncertain
World?...99
By Ken Alibek and Albina Tskhay

9. International Biological Defense and Verification 115
By Paula A. DeSutter

10. The U.S. Biodefense Strategy in the Time of COVID:
Reality Intrudes on Policy...129
BY STEPHEN A. ELLIOTT

11. Back to the Future: Biosecurity Lessons From the Late
1990s for the Year of COVID-19....................................137
BY JOHN LAUDER

About the Authors..151

Endnotes..155

Index..171

INTRODUCTION

By Fred Fleitz

"The United States is underprepared for biological threats. Nation-states and unaffiliated terrorists (via biological terrorism) and nature itself (via emerging and reemerging infectious diseases) threaten us. While biological events may be inevitable, their level of impact on our country is not."

> — Preface to *A National Blueprint for Biodefense: Leadership and Major Reform Needed to Optimize Efforts,* Bipartisan Commission on Biodefense, 2015

The 2020 pandemic caused by the novel coronavirus, officially designated "COVID-19" by the World Health Organization, highlighted a serious national security threat that most Americans were unaware of or dismissed: biological threats. Manmade pathogens that could be used as biological weapons are a security threat most Americans knew about. However, few understood the risk from naturally occurring pathogens and that some could be difficult for modern medicine to treat and cure.

While books and movies have portrayed pandemics caused by dangerous pathogens leaked from biolabs conducting research, few took this type of threat seriously. World leaders gave little thought to the ability of a dangerous

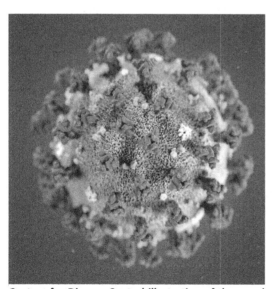

Centers for Disease Control illustration of the novel coronavirus.

and unknown virus spread by asymptomatic carriers around the world through air travel and did little to defend against it. Such ignorance about the nature of these threats left the United States and almost every other nation woefully unprepared to prevent the spread of the 2020 novel coronavirus within their borders.

The U.S. government was thoroughly warned that there were biothreats to the nation and that government at all levels was unprepared to deal with them. Congress tried to act on this threat by mandating in the 2017 National Defense Authorization Act that the Trump administration produce the 2018 National Biodefense Strategy. In 2015, the Bipartisan Commission on Biodefense, cochaired by former Senator Joseph Lieberman and former Homeland Security Secretary Thomas Ridge, produced a comprehensive assessment of growing biothreats, the lack of U.S. preparedness and leadership to protect the country against them, and a long list of recommendations to address U.S. biosecurity shortcomings. Most of the commission's recommendations were not implemented.

Other blue-ribbon commissions urgently recommending improvements to U.S. biosecurity suffered similar outcomes, including a report by the U.S. Commission on National Security/21st Century (Hart-Rudman Commission, 1999–2001); a report by the National Commission on Terrorist Attacks upon the United States (9/11 Commission, 2004); a report by the Commission on the Intelligence Capabilities of the United States Regarding Weapons of Mass Destruction (Robb-Silberman Commission, 2005); and a report by the Commission on the Prevention of Weapons of Mass Destruction Proliferation and Terrorism (Talent-Graham Commission, 2008).

Although numerous panels warned about U.S. adversaries employing pathogens as biological weapons, and about pandemics originating from dangerous viruses accidentally leaked from foreign biolabs, these panels did not address situations like the 2020 coronavirus. No panel predicted the lack of transparency that became evident when the Chinese government suppressed information about the coronavirus in December 2019 and January 2020, and retaliated against Chinese health care workers who tried to warn about it. The Chinese government also provided the World Health Organization (WHO) with false information about the infectiousness of the virus and pressed the

UN health entity to use this disinformation in official statements about the virus. Although the Chinese government implemented an unprecedented lockdown of 11 million people in Hubei Province on January 23, 2020, it did not halt international air travel from Wuhan, allowing the virus to spread worldwide. Chinese officials harshly condemned President Trump when he announced a travel ban on January 31 that blocked entry to the U.S. by any noncitizen or resident or family member who had been in China in the previous 14 days.

The Chinese regime's reckless handling of the coronavirus outbreak—which Senator Tom Cotton has called "criminal negligence"[1]—is a new variable in protecting the nation from biothreats. It represents a government's deliberate neglect of its commitments to the international community to be transparent about global health threats. This means the U.S. must expand its bio-surveillance efforts to cover the emergence of dangerous pathogens that some foreign governments will cover up or refuse to report. Better intelligence will be required to do this, as will international condemnations and sanctions against those governments.

The United States may be better prepared for future pandemics after the coronavirus pandemic of 2020. As has happened many times in the past, America usually increases its defenses after a battle because it tends to fight the last war but not prepare for the next one. Hopefully, biodefense measures implemented in response to the coronavirus pandemic will address the full range of biothreats; be comprehensive through all levels of government, industry, security agencies and society; and be permanent.

As this book goes to print, America is just beginning to end a national lockdown in response to the pandemic caused by the novel coronavirus. Over 112,000 Americans died from the virus as of mid-June 2020. Almost 2 million were infected. Although most made a full recovery, some incurred serious disabilities such as permanent lung damage. Others are suffering from a variety of lingering symptoms months after they supposedly recovered.

The virus did enormous damage to the U.S. economy, leaving 40 million Americans unemployed and an unemployment rate of nearly 20% at the end of May 2020. The U.S. government spent trillions of dollars on coronavirus relief legislation and programs. Many industries, such as airlines, restaurants, car-rental firms, and hotels, were devastated by the pandemic and may not recover for years. No one knows when or if a vaccine to protect against the virus will be developed, or whether there will be new outbreaks during the time it takes to develop a vaccine.

The outbreak of nationwide violent riots that followed the death of a man apprehended by Minneapolis police were not sparked just by police brutality. The social and economic costs of the 3-month coronavirus lockdown also fueled the riots. Organized and deliberate factors behind these riots, such as the role of far-left anarchist groups like Antifa, go beyond the scope of this monograph.

America's state and non-state enemies took notice of the social and economic damage and how it helped drive the worst rioting and looting in the United States since the 1960s. They now know that bioweapons can be an effective and cheap way to attack America from within.

The purpose of this book is to explain what we have initially learned from the coronavirus pandemic to prepare strong defenses. Eleven experts wrote chapters to discuss the full scope of the biodefense security threats to the United States. The views expressed in these chapters reflect those of the individual authors and are not necessarily shared by the Center for Security Policy or other authors.

The Chinese government's criminal negligence, deceptions, and cover-ups that denied the world crucial time that could have prevented or greatly curtailed this pandemic is a recurrent theme. We start our analysis with a detailed assessment of this issue by *National Review*'s Jim Geraghty and national security expert Gordon Chang. We are grateful to *National Review* for allowing us to reprint Geraghty's article about hazardous biological research conducted in Wuhan, China, laboratories on highly infectious coronaviruses endemic to bats, and how these viruses may have been leaked or otherwise inadvertently transferred from one of the labs to the Wuhan area, where it rapidly spread and became a dangerous pandemic.

Chang offers a similar analysis but also discusses the details of measures taken by the Chinese government in December 2019 and January 2020 to conceal information from the world about the true danger of the coronavirus and its high human-to-human transmissibility rate. Chang notes how Beijing silenced medical workers and "disappeared" some of them for trying to warn their colleagues about the extent of the danger. Chang also goes through the litany of other ways the Chinese government lied to the world and concealed information about this deadly virus. This included ensuring that WHO Director-General Tedros Adhanom Ghebreyesus would make false statements to dismiss or downplay the risks from this virus and mislead the world about the need to prepare proper responses.

Rosemary Gibson, a senior advisor at the Hastings Center and an expert in health care, health care reform, and patient safety, discusses another significant biosecurity issue: America's dependence on China for essential medical supplies and drugs. Gibson notes China's threats to withhold medical supplies and drugs during the virus crisis in retaliation for criticism of its mishandling of the pandemic. She also explains that many of the medical supplies sent by China to other countries during the pandemic, such as protective masks, were defective. Gibson says, as she argued in her acclaimed book, *China Rx: Exposing the Risks of America's Dependence on China for Medicine*, that it is urgent for the United States and the world to end its dependence on China for crucial medicines and medical supplies.

Claudia Rosett, a foreign policy fellow with the Independent Women's Forum and an award-winning journalist, discusses in depth how the WHO and Director-General Tedros mishandled the novel coronavirus by issuing false assessments of its infectiousness and by inaccurately praising Beijing for its initial steps to combat the disease. Rosett discusses how the WHO's disappointing record in addressing the coronavirus threat represents China's success in coopting the international organization, how the WHO mishandled other global health threats, and how institutional mismanagement and corruption has continued for years.

Two excellent analyses by former CIA operations officer Charles Faddis, Senior Director of the Jewish Policy Center Shoshana Bryen, and former Defense Department official Stephen Bryen explain the lessons state and non-state actors will draw from the coronavirus. Faddis discusses how terrorist groups may attempt to steal bioweapon agents from foreign labs. He surveys poor security at these labs and instances of security and safety problems at U.S. biolabs. These include the theft of anthrax samples, the discovery at one lab of long-forgotten smallpox samples, and the shutdown of a high-security biolab at Fort Detrick, Maryland, for biosafety violations.

Faddis concentrates on weaknesses of U.S. biosecurity and how U.S. enemies may exploit them. The Bryens offer a similar assessment as well as specific changes and improvements to U.S. responses to biothreats.

Next are two technical analyses of biological threats by two biowarfare experts, Dr. Ken Alibek and Albina Tskhay. Alibek is a former research director of the Soviet Union's biological weapons program and a world-renowned expert in the field of biological weapons and biodefense, acute and chronic infections, microbiology, and virology. Tskhay heads a scientific and analytical group evaluating the effectiveness of treatment methods and developing new biomedical products at Locus Fermentation Solutions.

Alibek and Tskhay first discuss uncertainty in differentiating between natural and manmade epidemics and the current state of medical defenses against them. They conclude that "the COVID-19 pandemic revealed an underestimation of the damage that can be caused by an infectious threat," which they believe indicates an urgent need for the development of novel approaches in biodefense.

In their second chapter, Alibek and Tskhay describe a possible epidemic caused by the deployment of a biological weapon and compare it with natural outbreaks, then discuss means to develop appropriate anti-epidemic, prophylactic, and therapeutic measures. Their chapter includes how an enemy might stage a biological weapons attack using the smallpox virus and a comparison of smallpox with COVID-19.

Former State Department Assistant Secretary for Verification and Compliance Paula DeSutter then weighs in by describing how international agreements prohibit biological weapons and how international organizations verify that nation-states are honoring their treaty commitments. DeSutter concentrates on challenges to verifying treaty compliance, the United States' method of conducting BW treaty verification, and indications that China has not fully complied with the Biological Weapons Convention.

In the next chapter, Stephen Elliott, a lawyer and former diplomat, discusses the Trump Administration's 2018 National Biodefense Strategy, which has five goals: risk awareness, increasing response capability, mitigation planning, sharing information, and economic and social recovery. Although Elliott gives Trump officials credit for producing a comprehensive approach, he faults the document for not being a strategy, but merely a detailed litany of things the government should do, things that it should analyze, and goals that it should aspire to meet.

This book's final chapter is by John Lauder, an independent consultant on weapons of mass destruction, nonproliferation, arms control, and intelligence. Lauder retired from the U.S. government with over 33 years of managerial, analytical, and policy experience in the CIA and National Reconnaissance Office and as an arms control negotiator. Lauder wraps up this monograph with an analysis of biological weapons proliferation and prevention efforts in the 1990s in terms of the coronavirus pandemic. He discusses efforts in that decade to raise public awareness of the growing bioweapons threat and efforts to produce improved intelligence to defend against it. Lauder concludes his chapter with recommendations for government action and leadership that are similar to those discussed by Elliott on the 2018 Biosecurity Strategy.

The authors of this monograph hope this work will educate the American people, elected officials, and policymakers about the growing threat from bioagents that the 2020 novel coronavirus pandemic represents. They intend for this analysis to play a role in developing and implementing a long-overdue comprehensive strategy at all levels of government to prevent bio-incidents, prevent their spread, and, if necessary, quickly and efficiently treat their victims.

The 2020 coronavirus pandemic exposed extensive U.S. biosecurity vulnerabilities and showed how easily a natural or manmade epidemic can result in huge numbers of fatalities as well as wreak havoc on America's economy and social order. We could be approaching a point—guided by the coronavirus pandemic experience—of a state or non-state enemy deploying a far deadlier pathogen as a biological weapon that could kill millions or billions, and possibly wipe out the human race. The U.S. government can no longer ignore this potentially existential threat to our country.

Fred Fleitz
June 26, 2020

7

1.

THE TRAIL LEADING BACK TO THE WUHAN LABS

By Jim Geraghty

There's no proof the coronavirus accidentally escaped from a laboratory, but we can't take the Chinese government's denials at face value.

It is understandable that many would be wary of the notion that the origin of the coronavirus could be discovered by some documentary filmmaker who used to live in China. Matthew Tye, who creates YouTube videos, contends he has identified the source of the coronavirus—and a great deal of the information that he presents, obtained from public records posted on the internet, checks out.

The Wuhan Institute of Virology in China indeed posted a job opening on November 18, 2019, "asking for scientists to come research the relationship between the coronavirus and bats."[2]

The Google translation of the job posting is: "Taking bats as the research object, I will answer the molecular mechanism that can coexist with Ebola and SARS-associated coronavirus for a long time without disease, and its relationship with flight and longevity. Virology, immunology, cell biology, and multiple omics are used to compare the differences between humans and other mammals." (*Omics* is a term for a subfield within biology, such as genomics or glycomics.)

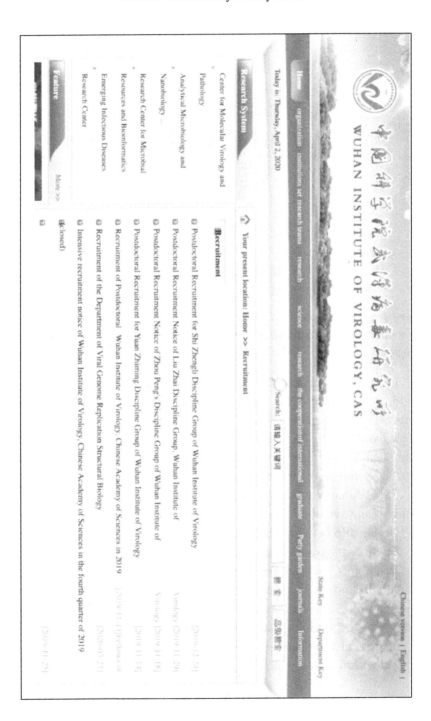

PI Introduction:

Peng Zhou, Ph.D., Researcher, Wuhan Institute of Virology, Chinese Academy of Sciences, and Leader of Bat Virus Infection and Immunization. He received his PhD in Wuhan Virus Research Institute in 2010 and has worked on bat virus and immunology in Australia and Singapore. In 2009, he took the lead in starting the research on the immune mechanism of bat long-term carrying and transmitting virus in the world. So far, he has published more than 30 SCI articles, including the first and corresponding author's Nature, Cell Host Microbe and PNAS. At present, research on bat virus and immunology is continuing, and it has received support from the National Excellent Youth Fund, the Pilot Project of the Chinese Academy of Sciences, and the Major Project of the Ministry of Science and Technology.

The main research directions of the research group:

Taking bats as the research object, I will answer the molecular mechanism that can coexist with Ebola and SARS- associated corona virus for a long time without disease, and its relationship with flight and longevity. Virology, immunology, cell biology, and multiple omics are used to compare the differences between humans and other mammals.

PI Introduction

Zhengli Shi, Ph.D., Researcher, Leader of Emerging Virus Group, Wuhan Institute of Virology, Chinese Academy of Sciences, Director of Emerging Infectious Disease Research Center of Wuhan Institute of Virology, Chinese Academy of Sciences, Editor-in-Chief, Virologica Sinica. Long-term research on the pathogenic biology of bats carrying important viruses has confirmed the origin of bats of major new human and livestock infectious diseases such as SARS and SADS, and a large number of new bat and rodent new viruses have been discovered and identified. So far in Nature, Science, Nat Rev Microbiol, the Cell Host Microbe, Nat Microbiol, PLoS Pathog and other SCI papers published journals 110 over papers, 2014 onwards for five consecutive years was selected Elsevier "China highly cited scholars' list (Immunology and Microbiology). Has won the "advanced worker" of the Chinese Academy of Sciences, the "May 1 Labor Medal", Hubei Province has outstanding contributions to young and middle-aged experts, Chinese Academy of Sciences "Excellent Graduate Instructor", French Palm Education Knight Medal and other honors. As the first person to complete the research on "Chinese bat carrying important viruses", he won the first prize of the 2017 Hubei Natural Science Award and the second prize of the 2018 National Natural Science Award. Elected to the American Academy of Microbiology in 2019.

On December 24, 2019, the Wuhan Institute of Virology posted a second job posting. The translation of that posting includes the declaration, "long-term research on the pathogenic biology of bats carrying important viruses has confirmed the origin of bats of major new human and livestock infectious diseases such as SARS and SADS, and a large number of new bat and rodent new viruses have been discovered and identified."

Tye contends that that posting meant, "we've discovered a new and terrible virus, and would like to recruit people to come deal with it." He also contends that "news didn't come out about coronavirus until ages after that." Doctors in Wuhan knew that they were dealing with a cluster of pneumonia cases as December progressed,[3] but it is accurate to say that a very limited number of people knew about this particular strain of coronavirus and its severity at the time of that job posting. By December 31, about three weeks after doctors first noticed the cases, the Chinese government notified the World Health Organization and the first media reports about a "mystery pneumonia" appeared outside China.[4]

Scientific American verifies much of the information Tye mentions about Shi Zhengli, the Chinese virologist nicknamed "Bat Woman" for her work with that species.

> Shi—a virologist who is often called China's "bat woman" by her colleagues because of her virus-hunting expeditions in bat caves over the past 16 years—walked out of the conference she was attending in Shanghai and hopped on the next train back to Wuhan. "I wondered if [the municipal health authority] got it wrong," she says. "I had never expected this kind of thing to happen in Wuhan, in central China." Her studies had shown that the southern, subtropical areas of Guangdong, Guangxi, and Yunnan have the greatest risk of coronaviruses jumping to humans from animals—particularly bats, a known reservoir for many viruses. If coronaviruses were the culprit, she remembers thinking, "could they have come from our lab?"
>
> ... By January 7 the Wuhan team determined that the new virus had indeed caused the disease those patients suffered—a conclusion based on results from polymerase chain reaction

analysis, full genome sequencing, antibody tests of blood samples and the virus's ability to infect human lung cells in a petri dish. The genomic sequence of the virus—now officially called SARS-CoV-2 because it is related to the SARS pathogen—was 96 percent identical to that of a coronavirus the researchers had identified in horseshoe bats in Yunnan, they reported in a paper published last month in Nature. "It's crystal clear that bats, once again, are the natural reservoir," says Daszak, who was not involved in the study.[5]

Some scientists aren't convinced that the virus jumped straight from bats to human beings, but there are a few problems with the theory that some other animal was an intermediate transmitter of COVID-19 from bats to humans:

Analyses of the SARS-CoV-2 genome indicate a single spillover event, meaning the virus jumped only once from an animal to a person, which makes it likely that the virus was circulating among people before December. Unless more information about the animals at the Wuhan market is released, the transmission chain may never be clear. There are, however, numerous possibilities. A bat hunter or a wildlife trafficker might have brought the virus to the market. Pangolins happen to carry a coronavirus, which they might have picked up from bats years ago, and which is, in one crucial part of its genome, virtually identical to SARS-CoV-2. But no one has yet found evidence that pangolins were at the Wuhan market, or even that venders there trafficked in pangolins.[6]

On February 4—one week before the World Health Organization decided to officially name this virus "COVID-19"—the journal *Cell Research* posted a notice written by scientists at the Wuhan Institute of Virology about the virus, concluding, "our findings reveal that remdesivir and chloroquine are highly effective in the control of 2019-nCoV infection in vitro.[7] Since these compounds have been used in human patients with a safety track record and shown to be effective against various ailments, we suggest that they should be assessed in human patients suffering from the novel coronavirus disease." One of the authors of that notice was the "bat woman," Shi Zhengli.

In his YouTube video, Tye focuses his attention on a researcher at the Wuhan Institute of Virology named Huang Yanling: "Most people believe her to be patient zero, and most people believe she is dead."

There was enough discussion of rumors about Huang Yanling online in China to spur an official denial. On February 16, the Wuhan Institute of Virology denied that patient zero was one of their employees, and interestingly named her specifically: "Recently there has been fake information about Huang Yanling, a graduate from our institute, claiming that she was patient zero in the novel coronavirus." Press accounts quote the institute as saying, "Huang was a graduate student at the institute until 2015, when she left the province and had not returned since. Huang was in good health and had not been diagnosed with disease, it added."[8] None of her publicly available research papers are dated after 2015.

Your present position: Home >> Notice

Wuhan Institute of Virology, Chinese Academy of Sciences

Source: Published: 2020-02-16 [Font Size: Tai Zhong small]

Recently, false information was circulated on the Internet, saying that our graduate Huang Yanling was the so-called "zero patient" who was first infected with the new crown virus. After verification, our firm solemnly declares as follows:

Huang Yanling graduated with a master's degree from our institute in 2015. During her studies, she studied the functions of phage lyase and the broad-spectrum antibacterial activity. She has been working and living in other provinces since graduation. Infection, good health.

At this critical moment in the fight against epidemics, related rumors have greatly interfered with our scientific research work. We reserve the right to pursue legal responsibility according to law. Heartfelt thanks to all sectors of society for their care, support and help!

The web page for the Wuhan Institute of Virology's Lab of Diagnostic Microbiology does indeed still have "Huang Yanling" listed as a 2012 graduate student, and her picture and biography appear to have been recently removed—as have those of two other graduate students from 2013, Wang Mengyue and Wei Cuihua.

14

Qiao Jinjuan   2012 PhD student

Huang Yaning   2012 graduate student

Li Heng   2011 PhD student

Wang Jing 2012 Graduate Student

Hu Yuanyuan   2011 PhD student

Zhang Yun 2011 Graduate Student

Her name still has a hyperlink, but the linked page is blank. The pages for Wang Mengyue and Wei Cuihua are blank as well.

(For what it is worth, the *South China Morning Post*—a newspaper seen as being generally pro-Beijing—reported on March 13 that "according to the government data seen by the *Post*, a 55-year-old from Hubei province could have been the first person to have contracted COVID-19 on November 17.")[9]

On February 17, Zhen Shuji, a Hong Kong correspondent from the French public-radio service Radio France Internationale, reported: "when a reporter from the Beijing News of the Mainland asked the institute for rumors about patient zero, the institute first denied that there was a researcher Huang Yanling, but after learning that the name of the person on the internet did exist, acknowledged that the person had worked at the firm but has now left the office and is unaccounted for."

Tye says, "everyone on the Chinese internet is searching for [Huang Yanling] but most believe that her body was quickly cremated and the people working at the crematorium were perhaps infected as they were not given any information about the virus." (The U.S. Centers for Disease Control and Prevention says that handling the body of someone who has died of coronavirus is safe—including embalming and cremation—as long as the standard safety protocols for handing a decedent are used. It's anyone's guess as to whether those safety protocols were sufficiently used in China before the outbreak's scope was known.)

As Tye observes, a public appearance by Huang Yanling would dispel a lot of the public rumors, and is the sort of thing the Chinese government would quickly arrange in normal circumstances—presuming that Huang Yanling was still alive. Several officials at the Wuhan Institute of Virology issued public statements that Huang was in good health and that no one at the institute has been infected with COVID-19. In any case, the mystery around Huang Yanling may be moot, but it does point to the lab covering up something about her.

China Global Television Network, a state-owned television broadcaster, illuminated another rumor while attempting to dispel it in a February 23 report entitled *Rumors Stop With the Wise*:

> On February 17, a Weibo user who claimed herself to be Chen Quanjiao, a researcher at the Wuhan Institute of Virology, reported to the public that the Director of the Institute was responsible for leaking the novel coronavirus. The Weibo post threw a bomb in the cyberspace and the public was shocked. Soon Chen herself stepped out and declared that she had never released any report information and expressed great indignation at such identity fraud on Weibo. It has been confirmed that that particular Weibo account had been shut down several times due to the spread of misinformation about COVID-19.[10]

That Radio France Internationale report on February 17 also mentioned the next key part of Tye's YouTube video. "Xiaobo Tao, a scholar from South China University of Technology, recently published a report that researchers at Wuhan Virus Laboratory were splashed with bat blood and urine, and then quarantined for 14 days." HK01, another Hong Kong-based news site, reported the same claim.

This doctor's name is spelled in English as both "Xiaobo Tao" and "Botao Xiao." From 2011 to 2013, Botao Xiao was a postdoctoral research fellow at Harvard Medical School and Boston Children's Hospital, and his biography is still on the website of the South China University of Technology.

www2.scut.edu.cn/biology_en/2017/0814/c5951a169022/page.htm

Botao Xiao

time: 2017-08-14

Botao Xiao

E-mail: botaoxiao(at)126.com or botaoxiao2011(at)u.northwestern.edu
Office: B6-405
Single Molecule Lab: B6-138

Education

Ph.D., Northwestern University, Evanston, IL USA, 2011
M.S. Chongqing University, Institute of Mechanics, Chinese Academy of Sciences, 2004
B.S. Chongqing University, 2000

Professional Experience

2017-Present Professor, South China University of Technology
2013-2017 Professor, Huazhong University of Science and Technology
2011-2013 Postdoctoral Research Fellow, Harvard Medical School, Boston Children's Hospital

Research Description

The Xiao group study mainly in the fields of cellular and molecular biomechanics, single molecule biophysics and engineering. Current research areas are: protein-ligand interactions, DNA and RNA assembly, high throughput nanometer measurements and manipulation, mathematical modeling and quantitative analysis. The experimental techniques include: magnetic tweezers, optical tweezers, biomembrane force probe, fluorescence microscopy, genetic engineering and chromatography. An instinct example is using high throughput single

At some point in February, Botao Xiao posted a research paper on ResearchGate.net, "The Possible Origins of 2019-nCoV coronavirus." He is listed as one author, along with Lei Xiao from Tian You Hospital, which is affiliated with the Wuhan University of Science and Technology. The paper was removed a short time after it was posted, but archived images of its pages can be found online.[11]

The first conclusion of Botao Xiao's paper is that the bats suspected of carrying the virus are extremely unlikely to be found naturally in the city, and despite the stories of "bat soup," they conclude that bats were not sold at the market and were unlikely to be deliberately ingested.

> The bats carrying CoV ZC45 were originally found in Yunnan or Zhejiang province, both of which were more than 900 kilometers away from the seafood market. Bats were normally found to live in caves and trees. But the seafood market is in a densely populated district of Wuhan, a metropolitan [area] of ~15 million people. The probability was very low for the bats to fly to the market. According to municipal reports and the testimonies of 31 residents and 28 visitors, the bat was never a food source in the city, and no bat was traded in the market.

The U.S. Centers for Disease Control and Prevention and the World Health Organization could not confirm if bats were present at the market.[12] Botao Xiao's paper theorizes that the coronavirus originated from bats being used for research at either one of two research laboratories in Wuhan.

> We screened the area around the seafood market and identified two laboratories conducting research on bat coronavirus. Within ~ 280 meters from the market, there was the Wuhan Center for Disease Control and Prevention. WHCDC hosted animals in laboratories for research purpose, one of which was specialized in pathogens collection and identification. In one of their studies, 155 bats including *Rhinolophus affinis* were captured in Hubei province, and other 450 bats were captured in Zhejiang province. The expert in Collection was noted in the Author Contributions (JHT). Moreover, he was broadcasted for collecting viruses on

19

nation-wide newspapers and websites in 2017 and 2019. He described that he was once by attacked by bats and the blood of a bat shot on his skin. He knew the extreme danger of the infection so he quarantined himself for 14 days. In another accident, he quarantined himself again because bats peed on him.

Surgery was performed on the caged animals and the tissue samples were collected for DNA and RNA extraction and sequencing. The tissue samples and contaminated trashes were source of pathogens. They were only ~280 meters from the seafood market. The WHCDC was also adjacent to the Union Hospital where the first group of doctors were infected during this epidemic. It is plausible that the virus leaked around and some of them contaminated the initial patients in this epidemic, though solid proofs are needed in future study.

The second laboratory was ~12 kilometers from the seafood market and belonged to Wuhan Institute of Virology, Chinese Academy of Sciences . . .

In summary, somebody was entangled with the evolution of 2019-nCoV coronavirus. In addition to origins of natural recombination and intermediate host, the killer coronavirus probably originated from a laboratory in Wuhan. Safety level may need to be reinforced in high risk biohazardous laboratories. Regulations may be taken to relocate these laboratories far away from city center and other densely populated places.

However, Xiao has told the *Wall Street Journal* that he has withdrawn his paper. "The speculation about the possible origins in the post was based on published papers and media, and was not supported by direct proofs," he said in a brief email on February 26.[13]

The bat researcher that Xiao's report refers to is virologist Tian Junhua, who works at the Wuhan Center for Disease Control and Prevention. In 2004, the World Health Organization determined that an outbreak of the SARS virus had been caused by two separate leaks at the Chinese Institute of Virology in Beijing. The Chinese government said that the leaks were a result of "negligence" and the responsible officials had been punished.

In 2017, the Chinese state-owned Shanghai Media Group made a seven-minute documentary about Tian Junhua, entitled "Youth in the Wild: Invisible Defender." Videographers followed Tian Junhua as he traveled deep into caves to collect bats. "Among all known creatures, the bats are rich with various viruses inside," he says in Chinese. "You can find most viruses responsible for human diseases, like rabies virus, SARS, and Ebola. Accordingly, the caves frequented by bats became our main battlefields." He emphasizes, "bats usually live in caves humans can hardly reach. Only in these places can we find the most ideal virus vector samples."

One of his last statements on the video is: "In the past ten-plus years, we have visited every corner of Hubei Province. We explored dozens of undeveloped caves and studied more than 300 types of virus vectors. But I do hope these virus samples will only be preserved for scientific research and will never be used in real life. Because humans need not only the vaccines, but also the protection from the nature."

The description of Tian Junhua's self-isolation came from a May 2017 report by Xinhua News Agency, repeated by the Chinese news site JQKNews.com:

> The environment for collecting bat samples is extremely bad. There is a stench in the bat cave. Bats carry a large number of viruses in their bodies. If they are not careful, they are at risk of infection. But Tian Junhua is not afraid to go to the mountain with his wife to catch Batman.
>
> Tian Junhua summed up the experience that the most bats can be caught by using the sky cannon and pulling the net. But in the process of operation, Tian Junhua forgot to take protective measures. Bat urine dripped on him like raindrops from the top. If he was infected, he could not find any medicine. It was written in the report.
>
> The wings of bats carry sharp claws. When the big bats are caught by bat tools, they can easily spray blood. Several times bat blood was sprayed directly on Tian's skin, but he didn't flinch at all. After returning home, Tian Junhua took the

initiative to isolate for half a month. As long as the incubation period of 14 days does not occur, he will be lucky to escape, the report said.[14]

Bat urine and blood can carry viruses.[15] How likely is it that bat urine or blood got onto a researcher at either Wuhan Center for Disease Control and Prevention or the Wuhan Institute of Virology? Alternatively, what are the odds that some sort of medical waste or other material from the bats was not properly disposed of, and that was the initial transmission vector to a human being?

Virologists have been vehemently skeptical of the theory that COVID-19 was engineered or deliberately constructed in a laboratory[16]; the director of the National Institutes of Health has written that recent genomic research "debunks such claims by providing scientific evidence that this novel coronavirus arose naturally.[17]" And none of the above is definitive proof that COVID-19 originated from a bat at either the Wuhan Center for Disease Control and Prevention or the Wuhan Institute of Virology. Definitive proof would require much broader access to information about what happened in those facilities in the time period before the epidemic in the city.

But it is a remarkable coincidence that the Wuhan Institute of Virology was researching Ebola and SARS-associated coronaviruses in bats before the pandemic outbreak, and that in the month when Wuhan doctors were treating the first patients of COVID-19, the institute announced in a hiring notice that "a large number of new bat and rodent new viruses have been discovered and identified." And the fact that the Chinese government spent six weeks insisting that COVID-19 could not be spread from person to person means that its denials about Wuhan laboratories cannot be accepted without independent verification.

2.

CHINA: THE COVER-UP OF THE GREATEST CRIME OF THE CENTURY

By Gordon G. Chang

"This is not the time for finger-pointing," wrote Cui Tiankai, Beijing's ambassador to Washington, in the *New York Times* in April 2020. "This is a time for solidarity, collaboration, and mutual support." The title of his op-ed says it all: "China and the U.S. Must Cooperate Against Coronavirus."[18]

Cui is right, unless the Chinese party-state deliberately spread the novel coronavirus, the pathogen causing COVID-19. If Beijing indeed intended to harm Americans, Washington would need to know that today. Among other things, malign intent would certainly make cooperation impossible as well as dangerous.

Unfortunately, the unthinkable is reality. I believe the evidence shows Chinese leaders took steps they knew or had to know would lead to the spread of the disease beyond their borders. In any event, their actions resulted in an extraordinary number of infections and deaths. At last count, the disease has spread to 214 countries and territories. This is the first time in history one nation has attacked all the others on the planet.

China's malign actions explain why Beijing has worked so hard both to prevent an investigation into the origins of the disease and to cover up evidence of wrongdoing. This chapter examines the Chinese cover-up and disinformation efforts.

We start with the rumors. Chinese rumormongers, among others, believe Beijing deliberately released the coronavirus from a laboratory in Wuhan, in central China's Hubei Province. Some say Beijing had an elaborate plan to kill off the elderly; others think the opponents of

Chinese ruler Xi Jinping released the pathogen to remove him from power. These and similar accusations are wild and almost certainly untrue.

Other theories point to a natural or engineered virus accidentally escaping from the Wuhan Institute of Virology or a nearby facility, a bat virus jumping to humans in a "zoonotic spillover" (anthropozoonosis) at a Wuhan "wet market,"[19] and a virus originating in southern China and somehow carried to Wuhan.[20]

It is not clear that anyone knows the truth about the origin of COVID-19, but one thing is certain: Beijing is determined to prevent foreign virologists, epidemiologists, and researchers from investigating the origins of the disease.

China's leader has made a show of cooperation. Xi Jinping told the 73rd session of the World Health Assembly, the WHO's decision-making body, in May,

> China supports the idea of a comprehensive review of the global response to COVID-19 after it is brought under control to sum up experience and address deficiencies.". "This work should be based on science and professionalism, led by WHO, and conducted in an objective and impartial manner.[21]

Xi's call for a review was not the result of a desire for transparency, however. On the contrary, he apparently intended to head off an independent and impartial investigation into the disease's origins and China's manipulation of the global health body. Earlier, Beijing had spurned calls from U.S., Australian, and European officials for investigations and threatened economic retaliation if they pursued their efforts.[22]

It's no wonder Xi wanted the WHO to lead the investigation. Beijing has held unusual sway over the UN body and has been able to prevent it from conducting a meaningful inquiry. There have been two WHO missions to Wuhan, the epicenter, since the outbreak of the disease, and neither accomplished much. A team went to the stricken city for two days in late January,[23] and another team participated in a trip to that and other cities the following month, from the January 16 to 24. Beijing maintains that in neither case did the WHO ask to visit the Wuhan Institute of Virology, the laboratory some believe was the source of the outbreak.[24]

Xi Jinping, in a meeting with WHO Director-General Dr. Tedros Adhanom Ghebreyesus, requested the second visit, what became known as the WHO-China Joint Mission on Coronavirus Disease 2019.[25] This was a China-friendly group: 13 of the 25 participants were from China, as was one of the coheads of the mission. There were only two from America.[26]

The mission split into two, and three members of one of the teams went to Wuhan for one day of activities on February 23. There, they visited a hospital and a mobile hospital as well as participated in a workshop with Hubei provincial officials and a "feedback meeting" with a health minister. The three members did not visit the wet markets or biological labs there.[27] It is not evident what any members of the mission learned in China. During the entire mission, no members went into the "dirty zones" in the hospitals treating COVID-19 patients.[28] As President Trump outlined in his May 18 letter to Tedros, Beijing did not allow the two American members of the WHO team to visit Wuhan.

The hastily issued final report on the February mission[29] is especially troubling. The report arrived at conclusions on matters, like the reduction in new cases, that WHO mission members could not have independently verified and, most revealingly, included language often found in Communist Party propaganda materials. "This WHO-China joint mission and its final report basically served as a staged performance to endorse the Party's handling of the COVID-19 pandemic," Xiaoxu Sean Lin, former lab director of the viral disease branch of the Walter Reed Army Institute of Research, wrote to me.[30]

Beijing has turned down many requests. The UN Food and Agriculture Organization asked to go to China to coordinate efforts to determine the origins, but was rebuffed. The WHO has requested information from China's Ministry of Science and Technology, which is leading China's investigatory efforts, but so far has not received anything.[31] On January 6, long before the outbreak became a pandemic, Washington asked Beijing to grant a U.S. Centers for Disease Control and Prevention team access to China, but Chinese officials denied this request and similar ones made that month.[32]

Chinese officials have been secretive about the Huanan Seafood Wholesale Market, the Wuhan wet market they once said was the source of the outbreak. The Chinese Center for Disease Control and Prevention in Beijing said it would create an epidemiological map of the market showing patients' known paths and where the animals were kept, but the map had not been released as of June 5, 2020. Beijing did not share with foreign countries samples taken on December 31, 2019, at the Wuhan market, and it destroyed animals taken from there. China has publicized the genetic sequences of "environmental samples" from the market but has withheld sequences of the animals.[33] One conclusion is evident: China deliberately destroyed and concealed evidence.[34]

Until a comprehensive on-site study is concluded, it is not prudent to rule out any theory about the origin of the coronavirus epidemic. Beijing could have facilitated an investigation but did not, and now it may be too late for an independent inquiry to find out much. Experts believe investigations should have been completed in December or early the following month.[35] In any event, local officials hosed the wet market with disinfectant, making further investigation there useless.

The blockage of an inquiry is in line with Beijing's months-long effort to conceal virus matters. Since the beginning of the outbreak, China's officials have devoted extraordinary effort to suppressing information and controlling the narrative. They evidently believe there is much to hide. Tellingly, their COVID-19 white paper, released in early June, is quiet about their actions before December 27.[36]

The Chinese Communist Party is guilty of more than silence, however, as the harassment of Dr. Li Wenliang and seven other Wuhan whistleblowers illustrates. These brave individuals comprising the Wuhan Eight were briefly detained in early January for warning of the coronavirus outbreak. They were accused of "spreading false rumors" and "disrupting social order." Li was forced to sign a statement expressing contrition, "an admonishment notice."

Beijing's efforts, however, backfired when Li passed away after contracting the virus, almost certainly as a consequence of treating patients at Wuhan Central Hospital. The first official announcement of his death, in the first week of February, sparked online outrage across China. State media, apparently to appease the public, then said he was alive but critically ill. Li was pronounced dead a second time, causing another uproar. Chinese censors scrubbed millions of social media posts supporting the doctor, who was only 34 years old when he succumbed.

Beijing, after a brief moment of openness in the wake of Li's death, is now back to warning doctors against "rumors." Moreover, through coercive tactics, the party-state has created other heroes in Wuhan, such as citizen-journalist Chen Qiushi, who mesmerized China—and the world—with his dry reports of the dire situation there, delivered from a bare room. Chen is among hundreds[37] who have been detained since the outbreak of COVID-19. As of June 2020, Chen had not been seen in public since authorities grabbed him in early February. China is holding collectors of coronavirus information in the notorious "black jails" and is silencing survivors.[38]

The Communist Party intimidates critics to prevent a free exchange of information. On January 26 it announced the inauguration of its special task force, the Central Leading Small Group for Work to Counter the New Coronavirus Infection Pneumonia Epidemic. There was only one public health official on the initial nine-person roster, which was heavy with political hacks, security personnel, and propaganda officials. The Party's propaganda czar, Wang Huning, was named vice chair.[39] Maintaining control of the narrative and, by extension, Xi's near-dictatorial rule, are evidently the Leading Small Group's primary goals.

Beijing's extraordinary efforts to enforce a single narrative inevitably raise one question: What is China trying to hide?

China's misdeeds look to be far worse than analysts have characterized them. Most critically, Chinese officials for weeks hid the fact that they knew the novel coronavirus could be transmitted from one human to another.

Beijing admitted human-to-human (H2H), transmissibility on January 20 when Zhong Nanshan, the famed Chinese pulmonologist, talked about two such transmissions in Guangdong province at a televised press briefing. The same day, China's National Health Commission officially confirmed the human-to-human spread of the disease.

Zhong admitted Beijing was slow to confirm the contagiousness of the coronavirus disease. A Harvard Medical School study suggests COVID-19 was infecting people in Wuhan as early as August 2019. [40] In any event, doctors in that city knew no later than the second week of December that human-to-human transmissions were occurring as there was no other explanation for the particular cases they were observing.[41]

Moreover, the evidence continued to pile up. Medical staff treating patients were falling ill in late December in at least two Wuhan hospitals.

Many of the initial patients, including the first diagnosed one, had no connection with the source then identified by central government officials, the Huanan market, thereby indicating those patients were probably infected by another human.[42] Beijing had to have known about the H2H transmissions in Wuhan shortly thereafter.

It would have been highly irresponsible if Chinese officials had said nothing about such transmissions during that crucial period in December and January, but they engaged in a campaign of deception. That effort began early in the outbreak. "The investigation so far has not found any obvious human-to-human transmission or infection of medical staff," the Wuhan branch of the National Health Commission stated on December 31. "The disease is preventable and controllable."[43]

On January 3, China's National Health Commission ordered Wuhan authorities to destroy samples of the coronavirus. In May, Beijing admitted it had issued such an order but said it was for safety reasons only.[44] This explanation makes little sense given that the valuable samples could have been preserved and helped researchers track down the virus and learn about its transmissibility.

Chinese officials announced a coronavirus outbreak only on January 9, two days after the *Wall Street Journal* did so. Even then, they understated the gravity of the problem. Peking University's Wang Guangfa told state media on January 10, in the words of the *Wall Street Journal*, that "the virus had little capacity to cause illness." On January 15, Li Qun, the head of China's CDC emergency center, downplayed the threat of human-to-human transmission.

This deceptive campaign was directed at the international community as well as at Chinese society. China's officials assured the WHO that H2H transmissions were not taking place, and as a result the WHO issued its now-infamous tweet of January 14 propagating China's false position. "Preliminary investigations conducted by the Chinese authorities have found no clear evidence of human-to-human transmission of the novel #coronavirus (2019-nCoV) identified in #Wuhan, #China," the tweet stated.

Even after finally admitting human-to-human transmissibility, Beijing attempted to play down the danger. Xi Jinping's first public statement on the epidemic, issued January 20, made no explicit reference to human-to-human contagion. That same day, Zhong, the pulmonologist, declared the coronavirus disease would not be as bad as SARS.[45] SARS infected 8,098 and killed 774 according to the WHO.

Chinese attempts to downplay COVID-19 were obviously cynical because, by January 21, the country in all probability already had a greater number of coronavirus infections. A Chinese virologist at about that time said the coronavirus outbreak "conservatively" would be ten times larger than the SARS one.[46]

Also on January 21, Xi Jinping tried to get the WHO's Tedros to "hold back information on human-to-human transmission of the virus" and delay a pandemic warning. The WHO denies the conversation took place, but the allegation, made by *Der Spiegel* based on information from Germany's federal intelligence service, the Bundesnachrichtendienst or BND,[47] fits known facts. Moreover, the BND's information looks consistent with the CIA's assessment, as reported by *Newsweek*, that China attempted to prevent the WHO "from sounding the alarm on the coronavirus outbreak in January—a time when Beijing was stockpiling medical supplies from around the world."[48]

China's sin was compounded because, while it first denied and then downplayed the possibility of human-to-human transmissions, it worked hard to prevent other countries from imposing travel restrictions and quarantines, especially by prevailing on the WHO to do its bidding. As the organization stated on January 10, "WHO advises against the application of any travel or trade restrictions on China based on the information currently available on this event." The critical words in this advisory are "on the information currently available," in other words, information supplied by China itself.

Beijing, despite adamantly opposing such restrictions in the early stages of the outbreak, established its own internal restrictions. Cities, including Beijing, imposed quarantines on arrivals from hard-hit countries,[49] and in late March, China completely banned arrivals by most foreigners.[50] Moreover, Beijing showed its belief that quarantines work when it declared "the biggest quarantine in history"[51] on January 23 with the lockdown of Wuhan and surrounding cities in Hubei Province. At one point, approximately 56 million people were under stay-in-place orders there.[52] In the middle of February, 500 million people in 48 cities and four provinces were in various forms of lockdown.[53]

So, while China's leaders knew the coronavirus could be passed from one human to the next, they tried to convince other countries that travelers from China could not transmit the disease and should be allowed entry. The inevitable result of their actions was to take an epidemic that would have been confined to China and spread it to the rest of the world, making it the deadliest pandemic in a century. Beijing's argument that countries should not ban Chinese travelers while maintaining its own lockdowns also suggests an intent to spread the disease beyond China's borders.

Moreover, there are indications Beijing tried to prevent the world from protecting itself. Chinese officials bragged that they quickly shared the coronavirus genome, saying they "wasted no time."[54] In fact, Professor Zhang Yongzhen's team at the Shanghai Public Health Clinical Center released the sequencing on January 11, but epidemiologists believe China could have shared genome data a week earlier. In fact, the Wuhan Institute of Virology had identified the new coronavirus and mapped its genetic sequence by January 2, and the next day the National Health Commission issued a secret directive prohibiting the Institute from publishing the genome.[55] Professor Zhang's team finished the sequencing on January 5.[56]

Zhang released the world's first genome sequence on two public platforms after it was clear that authorities were not going to warn the public. The day following the release, the Shanghai Health Commission shuttered Zhang's lab for "rectification." No reason was given for the action. The Level 3 lab had passed its annual inspection on January 5.[57] The Associated Press reported that Zhang's publication of the sequencing "angered Chinese CDC officials."[58]

As a "source with the center" told Hong Kong's *South China Morning Post*, "The closure has greatly affected the scientists and their research when they should be racing against the clock to find the means to help put the novel coronavirus outbreak under control."[59]

Advisers to the U.S. CDC, the Bipartisan Commission on Biodefense were concerned at that time that Chinese health officials had not released basic epidemiological data, hindering American and other efforts to contain the disease.[60] WHO staff, throughout January, were not getting the data needed to help understand the outbreak from Chinese officials.

Obviously, China's leaders did not want the world to be able to study the coronavirus.

We do not know what Xi Jinping and his fellow leaders in fact intended in December and January, but they saw how COVID-19 had crippled China. If they wanted to cripple other societies with the virus, they would have done exactly what they did.

Xi and other leaders took steps they knew or had to know would lead to the spread of the disease beyond their borders. There is only one explanation that fits the facts: they maliciously spread the virus to the world. This is a crime like no other. It is not just a "crime against humanity," it is a crime against all humanity.

Even China's lesser untruths had severe consequences and suggest bad motives. As has become evident—and as the U.S. intelligence community has concluded[61]—China intentionally undercounted the number of coronavirus cases. The inaccuracy was substantial. RAND estimates Chinese statistics in January undercounted the number of cases by a factor of 37.[62] This inaccuracy is so large that it could not have been the result of mere incompetence or negligence.

Beijing's low infection numbers lulled countries into not taking the precautions they would otherwise have adopted, creating a false sense of security. As Dr. Deborah Birx, the White House coronavirus coordinator, said on March 31 at the daily press briefing,

> I think when you looked at the China data originally, and you said, "Oh, well, there's 80 million people," or 20 million people in Wuhan and 80 million people in Hubei, and they come up with a number of 50,000, you start thinking of this more like SARS than you do this kind of global pandemic. So I think the medical community made—interpreted the Chinese data as, that this was serious but smaller than anyone expected, because I think probably we were missing a significant amount of the data, now that we see what happened to Italy and we see what happened to Spain.

Dr. Anthony Fauci, a member of the coronavirus task force, has also talked about being deceived by the Chinese.[63]

Surely public health officials elsewhere, convinced that the coronavirus outbreak was no worse than SARS, reacted the same way as those in America.

Beijing's downplaying of the contagion was substantial. In the middle of May, China reported approximately 83,000 infections and 4,600 deaths in the country. Neither figure is credible. A database maintained by the National University of Defense Technology, a Chinese military institution, included more than 640,000 updates in 230 cities from early February to late April, suggesting more than 640,000 coronavirus cases during that period.[64] In Wuhan, thousands of extra funeral urns were made available in late March as eight crematoria were reportedly running furnaces around the clock for weeks, suggesting the death toll was many multiples of that officially reported.[65]

Apart from an attempt to hide the deliberate nature of its attack on the world, Beijing may have been concealing the origin of the outbreak, perhaps because there was an accidental release. Analysts correctly point out that a lab leak is "an unverified theory,"[66] as Evan Osnos in the New Yorker called it, but there is circumstantial evidence[67]—and science[68]—suggesting a leak occurred.

Or perhaps Beijing is trying to shield the nature of activities at the institute from public view. The Wuhan Institute of Virology, which contains China's only Level 4 biosafety BL-4) laboratory, once bragged that it stored more than 1,500 strains of coronavirus.

It has also been engineering chimeric coronaviruses, as a 2015 article in Nature Medicine noted.[69] Even if the lab was not experimenting with viruses designed to specifically attack ethnic minorities, as Bill Gertz of the Washington Times[70] reported, Beijing may have much to hide at the facility,[71] such as a biological weapons program.

China is a party to the Biological Weapons Convention, which outlaws such programs.[72] In a clear signal that the Wuhan Institute of Virology was conducting military research, Beijing sent Major General Chen Wei, described as "China's top biowarfare expert," to head the BL-4 lab there in February. Chen, many speculate, was sent to clean up evidence of a leak or the existence of a weapons program.

Beijing may have had another motive for deceptive practices: extending Chinese influence. At first glance, spreading the disease makes little sense as it would undermine China's export-dependent economy by depressing demand for Chinese goods elsewhere. Yet disease-spreading would also "roll the dice," give China a chance to hobble rivals, and create opportunities to exploit. In fact, Beijing has attempted to do that with its "mask diplomacy," the purchase of goodwill with real and fictitious donations; its sweeping promise of a vaccine;[73] and its vicious disinformation campaign against the United States.

Yet the reality of Beijing's actions is far less benign. In an alert issued in mid-May 2020, the Federal Bureau of Investigation and a unit of the Department of Homeland Security warned that Chinese hackers were attempting to steal coronavirus treatments and vaccines, impeding medical research in the United States, and conducting a disinformation campaign against the United States.[74]

Beijing has been unrelenting in its attack on America. The campaign intensified in the beginning of February and has continued since. For instance, the Communist Party's *Global Times* gleefully told the world at the end of March that "COVID-19 Blunders Signal End of 'American Century.'"[75] Foreign Ministry spokesman Zhao Lijian, in a now-infamous March 12 tweet, even stated that the coronavirus originated in the United States and suggested the U.S. Army carried the pathogen to Wuhan. Zhao's comments were not isolated. "U.S. Is to Blame for Global Pneumonia Outbreak," screamed a headline in *People's Daily* Online in May.[76]

Xi does not accept the current international system of treaties, conventions, rules, and norms. On the contrary, he is attempting to impose China's imperial-era concepts on the world. The concept that underpinned the imperial tributary system was that peoples near and far were obligated to acknowledge Chinese rule. In short, China's emperors claimed they had the Mandate of Heaven over *tianxia*, meaning "All Under Heaven." A dictatorial state naturally thinks about the world in dictatorial terms, and *tianxia* is by its nature a top-down, dictatorial system.

Xi Jinping has employed *tianxia* language for more than a decade, but recently his references have become unmistakable. "The Chinese have always held that the world is united and all under heaven are one family," he declared in his 2017 New Year's Message. He has had his subordinates, especially Foreign Minister Wang Yi, propagate this bold narrative.[77] Xi has never had the power to compel others to accept this audacious vision of worldwide Chinese rule, but by striking down the United States with coronavirus, he almost certainly saw a historic opportunity.[78]

After Beijing unleashed the disease, it engaged in increasingly belligerent boat-bumping and other incidents against South China Sea and East China Sea neighbors; sent its troops into Indian territory; increased the tempo of dangerous intercepts of U.S forces in the global commons; and directed aggressive and provocative comments against many others, most notably Taiwan, Australia, and France. A Chinese ambassador even publicly suggested China absorb Kazakhstan, making it a Chinese province. With this new phase—the Chinese call it "wolf warrior" diplomacy—Xi's China has clearly moved into another period of territorial expansionism. Moreover, Beijing took steps to directly rule Hong Kong, effectively ending the promised "high degree of autonomy" under the "one country, two systems" formula.

In the meantime, China's wolfish diplomats have shown they can be charming when they think it is to their advantage. "What we are experiencing is a challenge of such magnitude that nationality and ethnicity should be irrelevant,"[79] Ambassador Cui wrote in his *New York Times* piece.

That statement seems correct, but it's unlikely Xi Jinping really views the world in that generous way. Washington should ignore the top Chinese diplomat in the United States when he tells us to refrain from finger-pointing or says we must show solidarity to, collaborate with, and lend support to his China.

China, after all, is ruled by a regime that has killed more than a hundred thousand Americans, caused the United States trillions of dollars in economic damage, and committed the greatest crime of this century, perhaps the greatest crime since the Second World War.

3.

LESSONS FROM THE CORONAVIRUS: DECOUPLE FROM CHINA TO STRENGTHEN BIOWARFARE PREPAREDNESS

By Rosemary Gibson

The world has watched as a coronavirus has killed hundreds of thousands of people, demoralized populations, destabilized countries, and devastated the economic security of nations. Adversaries are surely taking note of weaknesses in U.S. preparedness for biowarfare.

The pandemic has exposed America's dependence on China for essential medicines and medical supplies. Acutely aware of this dependence, China threatened to withhold drugs from the United States, an undisguised intent to kill American civilians in the midst of a global pandemic. A Chinese state-run paper editorialized:

> If China retaliates against the United States at this time, in addition to announcing a travel ban on the United States, it will also announce strategic control over medical products and ban exports to the United States. If China announces that its drugs are for domestic use and bans exports, the United States will fall into the hell of a new coronavirus epidemic.

Unleashing this threat would cause social disruption and death on a scale never before seen in America's homeland. Civilian and military health care systems, which account for approximately 18% of U.S. gross domestic product, would be powerless to care for the sick.

This is not the first time China has threatened to withhold medicines from the United States. More than a decade ago, one of China's domestic companies sold a blood thinner with a contaminant that was lethal in high doses and killed hundreds of Americans. The Chinese used their leverage to silence criticism by the federal government.

This chapter provides a brief overview of U.S. reliance on China for medicines, including medical countermeasures for biowarfare, China's strategy to disarm the United States and weaken its preparedness, and actions required for a minimum level of self-sufficiency to protect and strengthen the nation's health security, economic well-being, and national security.

BIOWARFARE AND MEDICAL COUNTERMEASURES

Biowarfare is the use of toxins or infectious agents, such as bacteria and viruses, with the intent to kill or incapacitate humans in an act of war. Medical countermeasures are life-saving medicines and medical supplies to prevent, mitigate, or treat conditions associated with biowarfare.

The release of a bioweapon coupled with control of the means of production of medical countermeasures is an especially potent combination to defeat an adversary.

The coronavirus revealed China's dominance in global production of medical countermeasures, including diagnostic tests to identify threat agents and personal protective equipment such as gloves, respirators (face masks), and ventilators. Its distribution of defective products reveals yet another tactical means to weaken the response of government and hospitals. For example:

- One million coronavirus testing kits sold to the United States gave inaccurate readings. The United Kingdom reportedly received 3.9 million defective testing kits from China, as did other countries.

- N-95 masks sold to the United States did not meet standards and failed to protect health care workers and other users from transmission of the virus.

- More than 9 million gowns destined for doctors and nurses in emergency rooms and intensive care units were found to be contaminated. Nearly 4 million packages of surgical instruments were similarly contaminated.

- Ventilators sold to the United Kingdom were reported by doctors to be defective and could cause patient harm and death.

The pandemic also revealed China's control over the world's production of the raw materials and chemicals needed to make antibiotics and thousands of other medicines. For instance:

- Azithromycin is a generic antibiotic that may be used for severe coronavirus cases in hospitalized patients affected by secondary bacterial infections. Hubei Province, whose capital, Wuhan, was the epicenter of the global pandemic, is a major source of the chemical components to produce the antibiotic.

- Ciprofloxacin is a generic antibiotic whose chemical precursor, 2,4-Dichloro-5-fluorobenzoic acid, is sourced only in China. This antibiotic is used to treat anthrax exposure.

- Piperacillin/tazobactam is another essential antibiotic. A single factory in China exploded several years ago and caused a global shortage. When the factory was rebuilt, the Food and Drug Administration (FDA) inspected the facility and determined the manufacturing process met U.S. standards. Three months later, the FDA's European counterpart, the European Medicines Agency, determined the company did not meet Western standards but allowed the product to be sold anyway to prevent life-threatening shortages.

Aside from antibiotics, China produces 90% of the raw materials and chemical ingredients in medicines required for the care of severely ill persons with coronavirus, including sedatives for ventilator use such as propofol, anti-inflammatories, and pressor agents to raise dangerously low blood pressure, among others.

China's dominance is global. A Dutch Public Television documentary aired in March 2020 reported on China's control over medicines in the Netherlands in the era of coronavirus. News stories in Australia, Canada, France, the Netherlands, and the Czech Republic reported concerns about reliance on a single country.

As demand for critical medicines surged in more than 100 countries, America was competing for the same medicines and the components to manufacture them. At least 75 countries, including the United Kingdom and half of the countries in the European Union, imposed export bans. The countries with the longest lists of drugs subject to temporary export bans have been Belgium, Czech Republic, France, and Poland, among others.[80]

India is the world's largest generic drug maker and produces 25% of U.S. generic drugs. The Indian government's Directorate of Commercial Intelligence and Statistics reported that the country's generic industry relies on China for 69% of the raw material and chemicals needed to make active pharmaceutical ingredients. India banned exports of 26 critical medicines in part because of its dependence on China, whose production shut down during the outbreak, hindering acquisition of key starting materials.

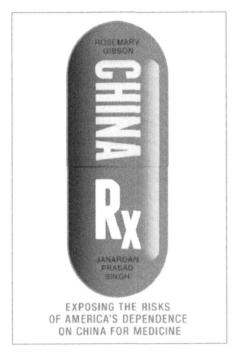

Every system is designed to achieve the results it gets. The current predicament, in which U.S. hospitals are rationing generic drugs and manufacturers are scrambling for the materials to make them, was predictable. As I noted in my 2018 book *China Rx: Exposing the Risks of America's Dependence on China for Medicine*, "a public health crisis could require the U.S. government to buy a large volume of drugs and it may have to stand in line behind other countries."[81]

BIOWARFARE COUNTERMEASURE PREPAREDNESS: THEN AND NOW

In 1988, Oak Ridge National Laboratory, a federally funded science and technology laboratory near Knoxville, Tennessee, implemented an emergency preparedness plan to ensure the continuous manufacture of antibiotics in the event of a nuclear attack on the United States. The names, addresses, and telephone numbers of manufacturing plants owned by 17 companies making penicillin, tetracycline, cephalosporins, and other antibiotics were carefully documented, along with a "how-to" manual to quickly rebuild or repair plants if they were damaged or destroyed in an attack.

Fast-forward to the September 2001 anthrax attacks, when letters with anthrax spores were sent through the U.S. postal system to congressional offices and media companies. To treat anthrax exposure, the federal government needed to buy vast amounts of doxycycline, a recommended antidote. Because the antibiotic was no longer produced in the United States, the government asked a Portuguese company to make sufficient quantities to treat 20 million people for 2 months. The company obtained the chemical starting material from its factory in China.

Today, Inner Mongolia is a locus of fermentation facilities. New plants are reportedly being built closer to Kazakhstan because of pollution concerns among residents. The FDA does not inspect antibiotic fermentation facilities that supply product for antibiotics sold in America. The agency inspects only companies that manufacture active pharmaceutical ingredients and finished drugs, which are the pills and vials of medicines ready for use.

How Dependent is the United States on China?

The extent of U.S. dependence was starkly apparent in 2015 when the FDA banned 29 products from Zhejiang Hisun Pharmaceutical Company, one of the country's largest manufacturers of active pharmaceutical ingredients. The agency had received 61 complaints from commercial customers alleging bacterial contamination and products that lacked full potency.

The FDA exempted 15 of the banned products because of concerns about drug shortages. Ingredients for antibiotics and chemotherapies to treat children and adults with cancer were among those exempted. The U.S. media reported that hospitals were rationing chemotherapies, but no mention was made of the reason, namely the concentration of global supply in a single country.

Testimony to the U.S.-China Economic and Security Review Commission by Christopher Priest of the Defense Health Agency in July 2019 highlighted the impact of the exposure on combat readiness.

> The national security risks of increased Chinese dominance of the global API market cannot be overstated. Pharmaceuticals are crucial to DoD's ability to promote the health of its Warfighters and protect them from nuclear, biological and chemical threats. Should China decide to limit or restrict the delivery of APIs to the U.S. it would have a debilitating effect . . . and could result in severe shortages of pharmaceuticals for both domestic and military uses.[82]

China celebrates its success in placing America in a position of dependence. In 2018, Chinese drug manufacturer Zhejiang Novus Pharmaceuticals argued successfully before a U.S. Trade Representative committee that its version of an antibiotic, vancomycin hydrochloride, should be removed from the list of tariffs. It stated accurately that tariffs on its product would threaten U.S. supply of a critical drug.[83] Chinese state television reported on U.S. reliance on the company and cheered the decision.[84]

CHINA'S CARTELS AND LAWFARE TO DISARM THE UNITED STATES

China has engaged in a concerted strategy to disarm the United States and inhibit its preparedness for biowarfare. Its cartels, government subsidies to domestic industries, and lawfare are among the means used to strip away U.S. self-sufficiency.

The Penicillin Cartel. A case in point is U.S. industrial capacity to produce penicillin. Bristol Myers Squibb owned the last U.S. penicillin fermentation plant, located in Syracuse, New York, and announced its closure in 2004. This was the year when China's penicillin cartel dumped product on the global market at below-market prices. Competitors in the United States, India, and other countries were driven out of business. Prices spiked after Chinese firms dominated the global market.

The magnitude of the loss to the nation's industrial base cannot be overstated. At one time the plant produced 70% of the world's supply. The closure involved the demolition of 50 buildings that housed complex operations and employed highly skilled chemists and pharmaceutical engineers.

As the Chinese government subsidized its domestic companies to manufacture other antibiotics, virtually all generic antibiotic production capacity in the United States was shut down. America is unable to produce medicines for bacterial infectious diseases including pneumonia, sexually transmitted diseases, superbugs, and sepsis.

Lawfare. China's lawfare strategy has used the U.S. federal courts to legitimize its cartels. The vitamin C cartel is a test case to undermine the free market system and has been ongoing for more than 15 years.

In the early 2000s, companies in China that produced ascorbic acid formed a cartel that fixed prices and controlled exports. U.S. purchasers that were adversely affected by dramatic price increases sued the Chinese companies for antitrust violations and presented overwhelming evidence of collusion. A Brooklyn jury found the companies guilty of violating the Sherman Act.

Chinese companies appealed the decision and the Chinese Ministry of Commerce filed a brief asserting that Chinese law required its domestic companies to fix prices and control exports and they were not required to abide by U.S. law. The federal appeals court vacated the lower court's judgment, noting that the Chinese firms faced a conflict between China's law and U.S. law. The court said that given the conflict, China's interests take precedence over any antitrust enforcement interests the United States may have.

In April 2018, U.S. purchasers appealed to the U.S. Supreme Court. In a unanimous decision 2 months later, the court vacated the appellate court's judgment and remanded the case for renewed consideration. Justice Ruth Ginsburg wrote that the appellate court gave too much deference to the Chinese government's statement that it required its companies by law to fix prices, and did not consider evidence presented at trial that raised questions about whether the practices were conducted as a matter of law or were voluntary. The appellate court has yet to render a decision.

WEAPONIZATION OF MEDICAL COUNTERMEASURES

The Chinese government has exhibited a pattern of deliberate and dangerous manipulation of drugs sold in the United States and other countries for economically motivated reasons.

As previously noted, hundreds of Americans died from a highly sophisticated scheme to insert a fake substitute for the authentic component in the blood thinner heparin, whose use is ubiquitous in civilian and military hospitals. The fake substitute was reportedly patented by the Chinese government and was undetected by quality tests commonly conducted in 2007 and 2008, when the deaths occurred.

In a similar scheme, a Chinese manufacturer used a cheaper chemical process to produce the blood pressure medicine valsartan. It yielded a carcinogen found in the production of rocket fuel whose levels were more than 200 times the acceptable limit per pill. The product had been on the market for at least 4 years before the carcinogens came to light.

The FDA did not initially detect these contaminations. Doctors and a pharmaceutical company, respectively, identified and reported them to the agency. The FDA lacks testing capability to ensure the quality and safety of every batch of medicine sold in the United States. Manufacturers are accountable for quality, but enforcement is far from stringent.

Medical countermeasures are not immune to China's weaponization. Medicines can be made with lethal contaminants or sold without any real medicine in them, rendering them ineffective. Products can be distributed to specific targets. Detection is time-consuming at best, and nearly impossible at worst.

Until such time that America can attain self-sufficiency, testing to detect poor quality and contaminated products is essential. More than 10% of generic drugs independently tested do not meet U.S. standards. A start-up company, Valisure, is reportedly the first pharmacy that chemically tests every batch of every medicine before offering it for sale. At its laboratory in the Yale Science Park in New Haven, Connecticut, medicines are rejected for not meeting quality metrics. Reasons for rejection include issues with dosage, dissolution, or levels of probable human carcinogens.

Looking ahead, the FDA is facing the beginning of the end of its ability to guarantee the quality and safety of medical countermeasures and other medicines imported from China. In early 2020, the FDA ceased foreign inspections to protect its employees from the coronavirus. Federal employees volunteer to travel to manufacturing sites. It may be many months, if not years, before inspections resume.

As tensions flare in response to China's handling of the coronavirus, China may not welcome U.S. government inspectors. It would not be the first time. Over the years, the Chinese government has made it difficult for the FDA to hire employees to work there by denying them visas.

DECOUPLE FROM CHINA FOR MEDICAL COUNTERMEASURES

The nation's security is only as strong as the weakest link. A root cause of U.S. vulnerability is procurement of medical countermeasures from a global supply chain intent on buying from the lowest bidder without regard for the nation's health security and national security. A minimum level of self-sufficiency is imperative.

To this end, the White House announced on May 14, 2020, that President Trump will sign an Executive Order providing the authority necessary to ensure the United States produces critical medicines and supplies for the country's strategic stockpiles. The aim is to increase the supply of essential items, use predictive analytics to forecast needs, deploy technology to provide real-time visibility of supply chains, and reduce dependence on foreign supplies.

It has been reported that the Executive Order will encourage the U.S. government, including the Department of Defense, Department of Health and Human Services, Department of Veterans Affairs, and Federal Emergency Management Agency (FEMA) to use taxpayer dollars to procure U.S.-made medicines and help rebuild the domestic manufacturing base.

Remarkably, special interests oppose U.S. production of medical countermeasures. Outsourcing to China with its state-subsidized prices is attractive to firms that profit from larger margins. This stance renders Americans and their government dependent on a country that has threatened to withhold medicines and supplies in an hour of need.

Rebuilding a sustainable industrial base requires long-term contracts with manufacturers that enable them to invest in their U.S.-based facilities and maintain an uninterrupted supply of quality medicines. Manufacturers should be paid a fair and transparent price, not a race-to-the-bottom price nor a price that does a disservice to American taxpayers.

Investments in advanced manufacturing of generic drugs enable production that is faster and cheaper, with real-time quality control and a smaller environmental footprint. Priority should be given to advanced manufacturing of active ingredients using continuous processes for the most critical medicines, including medical countermeasures and products for which China is the sole supplier. Once the initial capital investment is made, the cost to make finished drug products can be up to 40% less than the cost of traditional batch processing.

To be better prepared for the next pandemic or natural disaster, active pharmaceutical ingredients can be made using continuous processes and stockpiled for future use. They have longer shelf stability than finished drugs. When the next emergency occurs, stand-by manufacturing facilities can use stockpiled active ingredients to produce finished drugs within weeks, avoiding the kinds of shortages that have made the coronavirus response more challenging.

Commitments from private sector purchasers of medicines, such as hospitals and health systems, to buy generic products using active ingredients manufactured in the United States will demonstrate commercial viability and broaden the customer base beyond government.

Civica Rx, a nonprofit formed by the Mayo Clinic and 1,300 other hospitals that represents one-third of licensed hospital beds in the U.S., is using procurement dollars to buy essential medicines in shortage made with active ingredients produced in trustworthy countries. Federal investment in more efficient advanced manufacturing of critical generic drugs is likely to attract private investment.

CONCLUSION

The centralization of the global supply chain of medicines in a single country, whatever country it may be, makes it vulnerable to interruption, whether by mistake or design. Diversification of the manufacturing base is a strategic necessity.

The United States is not alone in reassessing its supply chains. Japan is working with more than 400 of its domestic firms to curb reliance on generic drugs and protective gear imported from China. The EU Commission and industry are discussing a plan to reinvigorate production of active pharmaceutical ingredients in Europe.

In America, the public and private sectors can reinvigorate manufacturing to achieve a minimum level of self-sufficiency required for the functioning of the health care system in the best of times and strengthen preparedness for biowarfare in the worst of times.

4.

A CHINESE COMMUNIST VIRUS AT THE WORLD HEALTH ORGANIZATION

By Claudia Rosett

I n an understated message on the last day of 2019, China notified the WHO of an outbreak of pneumonia of "unknown cause" in the city of Wuhan. So began the WHO's involvement in one of the most lethal deceptions of modern times. As it turned out, China had enlisted the help of the United Nations health agency not to contain the outbreak, but to help cover it up. For almost three weeks, while China's Communist Party enforcers silenced Chinese doctors, ordered laboratories to destroy specimens, underreported the rapidly rising case numbers, and insisted there was no serious danger of contagion, the role that Beijing assigned to the WHO was to nod along with whatever the regime said and reassure the world that the Communist Party's lies were true.

And lying for China is exactly what the WHO did, dutifully carrying on for months. Top WHO officials, especially Director-General Tedros Adhanom Ghebreyesus, praised Xi Jinping's

Dr Tedros Adhanom Ghebreyesus
Director-General
World Health
Organization

laggard actions as swift, his regime's dummied data as accurate, and his censorship as transparent. Assuming the WHO top brass have any ability to distinguish fact from fiction—which they surely do—their priorities appeared to have less to do with disease control than with legitimizing the actions of China's ruling Communist Party, the CCP, whatever those might be.

AIDING AND ABETTING CHINA'S CORONAVIRUS COVERUP

Mendacity and malfeasance are not new within the United Nations system. But rarely, if ever, have these failings converged to such globally devastating effect as they did in the WHO's handling of China's coronavirus outbreak. Operating since 1948 as a specialized UN agency, the WHO is tasked with promoting and safeguarding world health. One of the WHO's most vital missions is to monitor potentially deadly outbreaks, alert the world swiftly to any danger, provide useful information, and coordinate a response. Quite likely, lives depend on it.

Thus, during the critical early phase of the Wuhan outbreak, when the virus might still have been contained inside China, the world looked to the WHO for information and guidance. The WHO delivered dangerously misleading CCP reassurances, repackaged under a UN label. The most notorious example is a message it released on January 14, on Twitter: "Preliminary investigations conducted by the Chinese authorities have found no clear evidence of human-to-human transmission."

This statement is both artfully hedged (attributing the information to Chinese authorities) and profoundly misleading (the main message still comes down to "don't be too worried, this bug really isn't very contagious"). In the main, the WHO's lies did not reside in China's propaganda per se, but in appearing to endorse it, thereby legitimizing the lies. Had China's state propaganda mills simply tweeted directly that the virus was not very contagious, they might have drawn more skepticism. But channeled via the WHO, China's mortally dangerous malarkey carried a whiff of due diligence. As it turns out, that was wrong.

While the WHO was putting its imprimatur on Beijing's fictions, the disease was spreading from China around the globe, seeding what quickly became the most destructive pandemic in a century. Given what we now know about the infection rates of this virus, it's clear that China's authorities—even as they reported no new cases to the WHO for almost

2 weeks in the first half of January—had to know they had a nasty problem on their hands. We can only guess whether they allowed the virus to spread through sheer bungling, as Beijing tried to signal by blaming provincial officials, or whether Beijing unleashed the virus by malicious design, as Gordon Chang suggests earlier in this monograph, on the theory that if China was going to take a big hit from this plague, Beijing would level the playing field by ensuring the rest of the world shared the misery.

Whatever the inner workings, China's dictator, President Xi Jinping, eventually let it be known that in secret proceedings on January 7, just a week after China notified the WHO about the coronavirus, Xi himself had personally taken direct charge of dealing with the outbreak. Evidently, he then decided to let the festival of infection carry on for almost 2 more weeks, including a communal potluck dinner for some 40,000 families in Wuhan on January 18 and the travel of huge numbers of people out of Wuhan in advance of the Chinese lunar new year holiday.

Some of those travelers from Wuhan were heading abroad, but if their destination countries had any worries about such visitors bringing the virus, they could take comfort in the main sound bite of the WHO's January 14 tweet: no clear evidence of person-to-person transmission.

On January 20, by which time cases had appeared in Thailand, Japan, and South Korea as well as Shanghai, Beijing, and Guangdong Province, China's authorities suddenly reversed course and announced that the new coronavirus was, after all, passing from human to human. Three days later, on January 23, China's government imposed what was at that stage the largest quarantine in history, slamming a lockdown on all of Wuhan, a city of 11 million people, which then expanded to quarantines affecting hundreds of millions more.

TEDROS PRAISES XI'S HANDLING OF VIRUS AND BASHES TRUMP

The Wuhan lockdown looked like the moment for the WHO to finally sound a world alarm, by declaring what is known as a Public Health Emergency of International Concern (PHEIC). But, no, the WHO delayed while Tedros flew to Beijing for tea and a chat with Xi Jinping. Upon his return to the WHO headquarters in Geneva, Tedros held a press conference at which he made no mention of how badly Xi had misled the

WHO and the world. Instead, he rolled out a new role for Xi (no longer the douanier of a merely domestic virus), casting him as a champion of global disease control. Tedros praised Xi for his "very rare leadership" and suggested it was only due to the Chinese government's "extraordinary steps" that the spread abroad had been limited to what was by then "only" 68 cases in 15 countries. Tedros suggested that China, for its efforts, "deserves our gratitude and respect."

The next day, January 30—having waited a full 10 days after China's admission that the virus could indeed spread from person to person, and almost a month after the official notification of the outbreak—Tedros finally declared a global health emergency, the much-delayed PHEIC. By then, the number of confirmed cases in China had soared to 7,726, and the number abroad had jumped to 98 cases in 18 countries. On this occasion, Tedros told the media that the speed with which China had detected the outbreak and sequenced and shared the genome was "very impressive and beyond words."

Toward President Trump, and America generally, the WHO was less accommodating. While Tedros was praising Beijing for its abrupt, draconian lockdowns, he was simultaneously urging the rest of the world to keep travel open with China. On February 3, in response to President Trump's ban on flights from China to the United States, Tedros said there was no need for measures that "unnecessarily interfere with international trade" to prevent the spread of the virus. In Europe, which followed the WHO's advice, the open travel policy fueled the next massive outbreak. Not until March 11 did Tedros raise the level of international alarm by declaring the outbreak a pandemic. By that time, Northern Italy had succeeded Wuhan as the world's worst hot spot.

In America, where President Trump had imposed restrictions on air traffic with China over the objections of both the WHO and Beijing, the WHO's criticism of this move stirred up enormous controversy. In the meantime, the outbreak in Europe spilled into the United States and left America grappling on a bruising scale with the coronavirus.

TEDROS INVENTS NAME FOR VIRUS TO DEFLECT BLAME FROM CHINA

Prior to that, on February 11, Tedros had already done Xi another favor, bestowing on the coronavirus a name the WHO had specifically invented to avoid imputing any blame to China for the pestilence. Tedros announced that the virus had been officially dubbed SARS-CoV-2, and the disease it produced would go by the deliberately bland and easy-to-remember name of COVID-19 (shorthand for "coronavirus disease" and year "2019," when the outbreak emerged in Wuhan).

On February 26, Tedros made a further point of divorcing China from COVID-19, announcing at a WHO press conference: "Yesterday, the number of new cases reported outside China exceeded the number of new cases in China for the first time." That might sound like a casual observation, but it was right about that same juncture that Chinese state media and officials began insinuating that the virus originated not in China, but in the United States. This led, by late March, to Chinese Foreign Ministry Spokesman Zhao Lijian posting a series of questions on Twitter, clearly aimed at stoking rumors and implying that the U.S. military had brought the virus to China in late 2019 while attending the Military World Games in Wuhan. An example of one of Zhao's tweets is below.

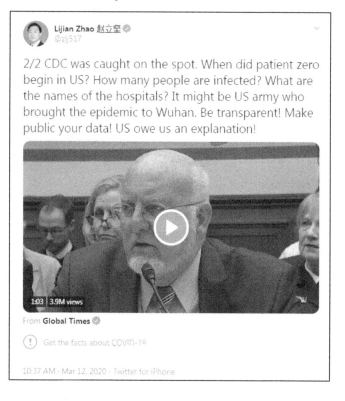

THE WHO'S POTEMKIN VIRUS INSPECTION OF CHINA

The WHO's accommodating ways with China's despotic regime also went on display when it sent a mission to China in mid-February to learn more about COVID-19. It was not actually an independent mission, but a "WHO-China Joint Mission," staffed by 13 international experts and 12 health professionals from China. To judge by the itinerary and resulting report, it had perhaps a bit too much in common with the Potemkin tours once offered by the USSR's Intourist to gullible foreigners who wished to believe they were seeing authentic Soviet life. The team, or various subsets thereof, raced through at least seven locations in 9 days, during which they met with hundreds of people presenting information—but all effectively under escort (in China's massively controlled surveillance state). Two experts dispatched by the United States were included on the WHO team, but only three members of the WHO contingent were permitted to visit Wuhan, the epicenter of the outbreak, and only for 2 days. The Americans were not among them. There was no discernible effort to investigate the origin of the virus, no visit to the Wuhan Institute of Virology, and certainly no mention of the underground videos that Wuhan bloggers had been smuggling out past China's Great Firewall, showing people collapsing in the street, being welded into their homes, or dragged out screaming from their apartments to be forced into group quarantines. China's payola for choreographing this tour came in the form of gushing praise from the WHO team leader, Bruce Aylward, a Canadian, who told an interviewer, "If I had COVID-19, I'd want to be treated in China."

Tedros Follows Beijing's orders to shun taiwan

As models of COVID-19-control go, the standout example is not China, but Taiwan, a Chinese democracy of almost 24 million people who have managed to suppress COVID-19 without trading away their freedom. As of this writing, Taiwan went through the many months of the China-spawned coronavirus pandemic with fewer than 450 confirmed cases of COVID-19 and seven deaths, an extraordinarily low number. Taiwan's people remember the lessons they learned from the 2002–2003 SARS outbreak that began in China—another killer coronavirus. In that case, China hid the outbreak for months, until the virus finally spread to Hong Kong and more than two dozen other places around the globe, including Taiwan. SARS infected more than 8,000 people and killed 774 before fading away.

SARS was less contagious than COVID-19, but caused severe pneumonia with a much higher mortality rate. Wherever it struck, it left people scared. When Taiwan's health authorities saw items circulating online in December 2019 about pneumonia in Wuhan of unknown cause, they took steps immediately to prepare for a return of SARS, or something like it. They began screening air passengers arriving from mainland China and readying further measures. On the same day that mainland China notified the WHO of the outbreak, the Taiwan Centers for Disease Control also contacted the WHO, sending an email to ask for more information:

> News resources today indicate that at least seven atypical pneumonia cases were reported in Wuhan, CHINA. Their health authorities replied to the media that the cases were believed not SARS; however, the samples are still under examination, and cases have been isolated for treatment. I would greatly appreciate it if you have relevant information to share with us.[85]

For anyone versed in SARS, which the WHO certainly should be, Taiwan's mention of atypical pneumonia cases in Wuhan being put in isolation should have sent up a warning flare that this was potentially a highly dangerous outbreak, not to be covered up or shrugged off. This kind of forthright dealing and foresight is a testament that Taiwan, which held observer status at the WHO from 2009–2016, would be a valuable member of the WHO, more so in many ways than mainland China with its cover-ups, propaganda, predatory ambitions, and disquieting record of engendering killer coronaviruses. But China doesn't want an unsubjugated Taiwan at the WHO, so, to please Beijing, the WHO rejects democratic Taiwan—even as it makes room for the likes of North Korea, Iran, and China. The WHO's Bruce Aylward, the Canadian who said if he had COVID-19 he would want to be treated in China, gave an interview in April to Hong Kong's RTHK TV station, in which the reporter asked him several times if the WHO might reconsider Taiwan's status. Aylward refused to answer, first hanging up, and when the reporter called back, simply brushing aside the question.

On April 8, Tedros took an even nastier attitude toward Taiwan. At a press briefing in which he lauded the WHO for various accomplishments during the coronavirus pandemic and called for "countries and partners to bring the world together," Tedros then singled out Taiwan for insult and attack. His remarks implied that people from Taiwan had been sending him racist slurs because he is from Africa. He presented no evidence of any kind, so there was nothing concrete for Taiwan to refute. Taiwan's President Tsai Ing-wen responded with a Facebook Post inviting Tedros to come visit Taiwan. She wrote to Tedros, "Taiwan has always opposed all forms of discrimination," and added, "For years we have been excluded from international organizations and we know better than anyone else what it feels like to be discriminated against and isolated."

XI TRIES TO CHANGE THE NARRATIVE ABOUT THE PANDEMIC AT MAY 2020 WHO ANNUAL MEETING

By May 2020, China had been subjected to growing international criticism for its mishandling of the coronavirus. U.S. officials, especially President Trump and Secretary of State Mike Pompeo, were claiming that Beijing's deceptions about the virus and withholding of information were responsible for its spread in the United States. By that time, Australia was calling for an independent investigation of the origin of the virus in Wuhan. There were calls from the United States, Germany, and the United Kingdom for China to pay billions of dollars in compensation for its negligent handling of the pandemic.

Chinese officials attempted to change the global narrative about the coronavirus pandemic at the WHO's annual World Health Assembly on May 18, 2020 (held online, in the era of COVID-19), to portray China in a positive light and prevent any independent and intrusive investigation of the virus origins in China.

Chinese President Xi Jinping appeared as the star speaker at the WHO meeting and made news when he said China would provide $2 billion over two years "to help with COVID-19 response." But Xi did not say these funds would be given to the WHO. Rather, China plans to spend those funds on "economic and social development in affected countries, especially developing countries." The way Xi's CCP works, it would be no great surprise if those funds are spent not on impoverished and sick human beings, but on more debt trap diplomacy for China to acquire, say, another port. Xi's offer sounded more like a bid to advance China's dreams of moving toward world domination than help for the WHO's mission of promoting health.

President Xi also made news at the WHO meeting by appearing to reverse himself, agreeing to an "objective and impartial" investigation into the origins of the virus and the global response, including by the WHO. But Xi did not actually concede anything because World Health Assembly members voted for a resolution approving an investigation by the WHO—which is beholden to Beijing—and not an independent investigation as demanded by Australia and other countries. Neither China nor any other nation was mentioned in this resolution. Xi agreed to cooperate with this investigation "once the health emergency ends," which could be years in the future.

Xi also proposed that China work with the UN "to set up a global humanitarian and response depot and hub in China." This might be handy for Xi if he's planning to let loose more pandemics, but it's not clear why the UN should be involved—unless he's hoping that America, via its contributions to the UN system, will help pay for it.

Xi used the May 2020 World Health Assembly meeting to generate positive press for China with deceptive offers of aid to fight the virus and agreement to a significantly watered-down proposal to investigate its origins. Xi's efforts were at least partially successful because he played off widespread opposition by WHO members to President Trump's threats to cut off funding to the WHO and withdraw from the organization.

TRUMP CALLS OUT WHO FOR BEING BEIJING'S PUPPET

By April, after more than three months of watching the WHO perform as a shill for China's Communist Party, President Trump developed doubts about the benefits of supporting this organization. On April 14, Trump announced he was suspending U.S. funding to the WHO, pending a 30-day review of what had gone wrong. On May 18 he sent an open letter to Tedros, noting among other things that Tedros had delayed declaring a pandemic until the virus "had killed more than 4,000 people and infected more than 100,000 in at least 114 countries around globe." Trump wrote, reasonably enough, that "The only way forward for the World Health Organization is if it can actually demonstrate independence from China." Trump warned that if the WHO did not "commit to substantive improvements within 30 days," he would make the U.S. funding freeze permanent and reconsider U.S. membership in the organization.

During the mid-May WHO World Health Assembly, President Trump said about the WHO: "They're a puppet of China, they're China-centric."

On May 29, with no sign from the WHO of any plans to downsize China's dominant role, Trump announced he was terminating the U.S. relationship with the WHO. He detailed that "China has total control over the World Health Organization, despite paying only $40 million per year compared to what the United States has been paying, which is approximately $450 million a year." He said the United States will be "redirecting those funds to other worldwide and deserving, urgent, global public health needs."

There's been a lot of hand-wringing over this by people who regard the WHO as a permanent world fixture, deserving of support if only because global health sounds awfully good—especially during a pandemic. But perhaps today's WHO is not the ideal vehicle for such goals. It's highly unlikely that in any short or medium term the WHO can be reformed. Tedros's current five-year term won't expire until 2022. In view of his performance during the current pandemic, China might be quite happy to help him win another. China's grip on the WHO has clearly reached the stage at which it will only loosen up if there is regime change in Beijing.

CHINA HAS COLONIZED THE WORLD HEALTH ORGANIZATION

China had been busy colonizing the WHO for years, well before Tedros took charge. This is part of a broad bid by Beijing to control ever more terrain within the UN and other international organizations. This campaign under Xi Jinping has now led to China running four of the UN's 15 specialized agencies: the Food and Agriculture Organization (FAO), the International Telecommunication Union (ITU), the International Civil

Aviation Organization (ICAO), and the UN Industrial Development Organization (UNIDO).

In the case of the WHO, China was effectively in charge from 2007–2017, for 10 years before Tedros became director-general. The WHO's previous top boss was Margaret Chan of Hong Kong, a semi-autonomous region of China (or it was until Beijing broke its treaty promises and rolled right over Hong Kong's legal system with a new national security law). Chan served as Hong Kong's less than entirely successful director of health during the 2002–2003 SARS outbreak that spread from China to Hong Kong. In 2004, Hong Kong's legislature voted to censure her for failing to respond quickly enough to "soft intelligence" about the SARS crisis brewing just north of Hong Kong's border.

As WHO director-general, Chan oversaw the appointment of Xi Jinping's wife, Peng Liyuan, as a WHO Goodwill Ambassador. She presided over the WHO's disastrously botched response to a major Ebola outbreak from 2013–2014 in West Africa. The WHO's failings on that occasion included—as with COVID-19 today—a damaging delay in declaring a Public Health Emergency of International Concern. The head of that WHO Ebola Response Team was the same Bruce Aylward who doesn't like to answer questions about Taiwan and regards China as a world leader in disease management. In 2015, a WHO panel investigating the agency's performance in the West African Ebola outbreak reported, "The Panel considers that WHO does not currently possess the capacity or organizational culture to deliver a full emergency public health response."

During Chan's final months at the helm of the WHO, in 2017, she hosted a first visit to the organization's Geneva headquarters by Xi Jinping and his wife. Tedros, a former health minister and foreign minister of Ethiopia, was then running his successful campaign, as China's favored candidate, to succeed Chan. Tedros was also backed by a bloc of African and Asian countries.

Tedros Adhanom Ghebreyesus was a controversial choice to head the WHO. He likes to be called "Dr. Tedros" but is not a medical doctor—he holds a PhD in Community Health. Tedros is the first WHO director-general in the organization's 72-year history who is not a medical doctor. His 2017 election as WHO director-general was described as "nasty" and he was accused by another candidate of covering up three cholera epidemics in Ethiopia when he was health minister. Tedros denied this charge.[86],[87]

In 2017, Tedros attempted to name then Zimbabwe President-for-Life Robert Mugabe a WHO Goodwill Ambassador in recognition of his supposed commitment to public health. Tedros praised Zimbabwe at the time as a country that "places universal health coverage and health promotion at the center of its policies to provide health care to all." Tedros was forced to withdraw this offer due to international outrage against the Zimbabwean dictator's abysmal human rights record and years of mismanagement of the country that caused the health care system to collapse. Commenting on this decision, "Several former and current WHO staff said privately they were appalled at the poor judgement and miscalculation by Tedros," according to *The Guardian*.[88]

There's at least one thing Chan and Tedros have in common, beyond Beijing's apparent appreciation for their style of running the WHO, with its 7,000 staffers and annual budget of more than $2 billion. Both Chan and Tedros appear prone to management styles that have inspired news coverage of the WHO's extravagant travel habits.

According to the Associated Press (AP), during the final days of Chan's tenure in 2017, the WHO "routinely spends about $200 million a year on travel—far more than what it doles out to fight some of the biggest problems in public health, including AIDS, tuberculosis or malaria." The AP article recounted that WHO staff were openly ignoring rules meant to limit travel costs. Chan herself stayed at a suite in Guinea costing $1,008 per night on a trip to congratulate health workers for beating Ebola.[89]

Apparently things are slightly leaner under Tedros, but not by much. Many WHO staffers still find ways to fly business class and bill it to the WHO, even when they not authorized for such travel. In 2019, the AP reported, "The World Health Organization spent nearly $192 million on travel expenses last year, with staffers sometimes breaking the agency's own rules by traveling in business class, booking expensive last-minute tickets and traveling without the required approvals." Noting that this represented a 4% decrease from the Chan era, the AP also quoted Sophie Harman, a global health professor at Queen Mary University in London, who said "The agency's inability to curb its expenses could undermine its credibility and make it more difficult to raise money to fight health crises."[90]

CONCLUSION

Fed up with the WHO's gross mishandling of the coronavirus pandemic, behavior as a Chinese puppet, and corruption, President Trump sent the world a powerful message when he cut off U.S. funding and withdrew the United States from the organization. It is unclear at this time whether Trump officials believe there is any real prospect that the WHO will implement reforms to address Trump's concerns or if they have concluded the WHO is irredeemable and should be replaced by a new international health organization.

For a variety of reasons, America's withdrawal from the WHO will not cripple the organization and is unlikely to lead to an alternative health organization. America's $450 million annual WHO contribution is only about 16% of the organization's budget. Other large, corrupt UN organizations like UNESCO have survived U.S. withdrawals. Moreover, the U.S. withdrawals were widely unpopular with WHO members, few of which are likely to follow the United States out the door. President Trump's withdrawal also fell under strong criticism from his political opponents, some of whom pledged to reverse his decision.

Nevertheless, the absence of the United States, the global leader in medical research, will be a sore spot for the WHO and will likely lead to pressure from many of its members for reforms. It remains to be seen whether the WHO will implement serious reforms and cease collaboration with the Chinese Communist government to convince the Trump administration to rejoin the organization.

5.

THE LESSONS TERRORISTS WILL DRAW FROM THE CORONAVIRUS PANDEMIC

By Charles Faddis

T errorists aren't interested in frontal assaults. They don't look to overwhelm your defenses. They walk the wire. They analyze. They watch, and they wait. Then they strike in a way that exploits your weaknesses, maximizes their strengths, and ensures the greatest chance of success.

From a psychological perspective, there can be no better example of this principle than the terrorist attacks on the World Trade Center and the Pentagon on September 11, 2001. For decades prior to these attacks, our focus had been on stopping the hijacking of civilian airliners by groups who then bartered the captive passengers for financial and political gain. Our policy was crystal clear. Offer no resistance in the air. Do whatever is demanded. Get the plane on the ground, where it will be in reach of hostage rescue forces.

Terrorists watched. Terrorists learned. Even a minimal amount of force would suffice to gain control of a jet airplane, a flying bomb.

In the same way, terrorist groups worldwide have watched what has unfolded around the world with regard to the ongoing pandemic. They have taken careful notes and are guaranteed to plan future biological terrorist attacks based on what they have learned.

HISTORICAL INTEREST IN BIOWEAPONS BY TERRORISTS: WHAT WE KNOW THEY HAVE TRIED BEFORE

Virtually every terrorist group on the planet today has at one point or another expressed an interest in weapons of mass destruction.

Perhaps chief among the various WMD capabilities sought has been a biological weapon of some kind. Widely regarded as the "poor man's nuclear weapon," biological agents hold out to groups lacking extensive engineering and manufacturing capabilities the possibility of being able to cause mass casualties with relatively crude capabilities.[91]

A 2015 report by the Bipartisan Commission on Biodefense said this about how easily accessible bioweapon agents are to state and non-state actors:

> The Department of State assesses that China, Iran, North Korea, Russia, and Syria continue to engage in dual-use or biological weapons-specific activities and are failing to comply with the BWC [Biological Weapons Convention]. Caches of incompletely destroyed or buried biological weapons materials from old state programs can now be accessed again by new state programs, and then smuggled to other regions for use in today's wars and by today's terrorists. Weapons that once consumed a great deal of time and resources to make now take far less, and it is reasonable to believe that what the United States could accomplish more than 40 years ago, others can accomplish now.

> The resources necessary to produce biological weapons are more easily obtained by states and terrorists than in years past. For example, regarding ISIS, former Representative Mike Rogers believes that, "the longer they have freedom of operation in any space that contains those kinds of elements, I think that's dangerous to the United States and our European allies." Additionally, terrorist organizations, domestic militia groups, and lone wolves have expressed intent to use and shown some capacity to develop biological weapons. Advances in science have led to a convergence of biology and chemistry, and an ability (through synthetic biology) to create and combine agents. All of this has expanded the number and types of potential biological weapons and made it more difficult to fully comprehend the enormity of the threat.[92]

When U.S. forces entered Afghanistan after 9/11, they found clear evidence that al Qaeda was working with anthrax and attempting to develop a biological weapon for future attacks. Fortunately, it appears the program was still in its infancy when America invaded. CIA Director George Tenet said at the time, "Documents recovered from Al Qaeda facilities in Afghanistan show that bin Laden was pursuing a sophisticated biological weapons research program."[93]

ISIS has long been known to have been working on biological weapons. It has experimented with animal matter and other potential hosts for deadly pathogens. Muhammed Abrini, an ISIS member behind the 2015 Paris attacks, was caught with a crude bomb constructed using animal matter, suggesting that he was actively working on weaponizing some sort of biological material.[94]

Press reports in recent years have indicated that MI5, the British internal intelligence service, is concerned about ISIS terrorists using both ricin and anthrax to poison supermarkets and contaminate water supplies and warned in 2018, "The use of chemical and biological weapons by Islamic State is a threat which is being treated very seriously."[95]

There has also been concern for some time about the possibility that Al Qaeda and other Islamic extremist groups may have succeeded in acquiring materials leaking out of Syria's bioweapons programs during the fighting in that war-torn country. Jihadists from a number of groups in Syria are known to have been actively seeking to gain control of the Assad regime's biological weapons stockpile. There was widespread looting of bio-pharmaceutical laboratories scattered across Syria.

Al Qaeda branches outside of Syria, in Yemen and North Africa, are also known to have attempted to obtain biological weapons in the past.[96]

In 2014, a laptop found in Syria in the course of fighting against the Islamic State was discovered to have instructions on it pertaining to the manufacture of chemical weapons and detailing attempts to weaponize bubonic plague. This laptop belonged to a Tunisian national who studied chemistry in his home country before joining ISIS in Syria.

> "The benefits of a biological weapon are that it doesn't come up often, and the losses are massive," said one file on the laptop. "When a mouse is injected by the bacteria, the

symptoms of the disease begin to show after 24 hours. It's best to use in places like underground trains or soccer fields and it can be used in a suicide attack as well."

Along with instructions on weaponizing the plague was a religious fatwa providing the religious justification for the use of biological weapons. "If the Muslims can't overwhelm the infidels in any other way, they are allowed to use weapons of mass destruction to kill everyone and erase them and their descendants from the earth."[97]

WEAKNESSES EXPOSED BY THE PANDEMIC

Unfortunately, terrorist groups have probably absorbed a great deal by observing the events that transpired during the coronavirus pandemic. These occurrences deserve special consideration:

Failures in lab security and practices combined with the proliferation of labs. For many years there has been concern about the proliferation of biolabs around the world and the difficulty of controlling access to the dangerous pathogens many are researching.

There have been many security and safety problems at U.S. biolabs. The Bipartisan Commission on Biodefense found in 2015 that "the U.S. government has mishandled extremely dangerous viruses and bacteria in some of its highest-level laboratories."[98] This includes a series of safety and security violations at the U.S. Army Medical Research Institute of Infectious Diseases (USAMRIID) in Fort Detrick, Maryland, one of only 13 bio-level 4 (BL-4) laboratories in the United States. In August 2019, research was halted at USAMRIID because it did not have sufficient systems in place to decontaminate wastewater from its highest-security labs, according to the *New York Times*. The *Times* also reported that in 2009, research at USAMRIID was suspended because it was storing dangerous pathogens not listed in its database. The *Times* article also noted that USAMRIID once employed Bruce E. Ivins, a microbiologist who was a leading suspect—but who was never charged—for the anthrax mailings in 2001 that killed five people. Dr. Ivins died in 2008, apparently by suicide.[99]

There were accidental releases of anthrax due to poor biosafety procedures from Russian laboratories in 1979 and from a U.S. military laboratory at Dugway Proving Grounds in 2015.

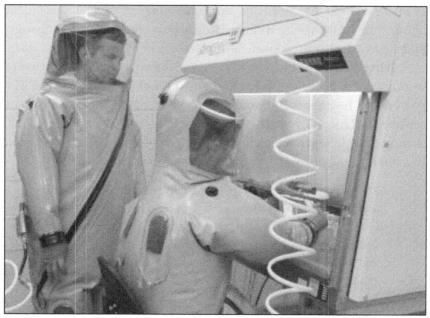

U.S. Army Medical Research Institute of Infectious Diseases (USAMRIID) at Fort Detrick, Maryland, conduct experiments with the Ebola virus in a BL-4 biolab. (USAMRIID photo)

A similarly serious biosecurity incident occurred in 2014 when a half-dozen forgotten vials of smallpox virus were discovered while cleaning out a storage area on the campus of the National Institutes of Health in Bethesda, Maryland.[100] Under an agreement with the WHO, only two BL-4 labs are permitted to retain stocks of smallpox virus: the CDC in Atlanta, Georgia, and Russia's State Center of Virology and Biotechnology (VECTOR) in Koltsovo, Russia.

Pathogens that terrorist groups may attempt to use as biological weapons will likely come from biolabs in other countries, where security and safety standards are much lower than in the United States.

Where, precisely, COVID-19 came from remains unclear. As discussed earlier in this monograph by Jim Geraghty and Gordon Chang, it appears very likely that it came out of one of two biolabs in or near Wuhan, China. What is beyond dispute is that procedures in those labs were dangerous and unprofessional. Control over dangerous organisms communicable to humans was tenuous at best.[101]

If an organism can escape from a biolab without assistance due to poor practices and shortages in trained personnel and equipment, it also could be stolen. The need for the establishment of an independent bioweapons program by a terrorist group is eliminated if dangerous pathogens can simply be taken surreptitiously or by force.

Cyberthreats to biosecurity. Terrorist groups could also attempt to carry out a biological weapon attack through cyber-espionage. The goal would be to steal information about a nation's biodefenses or sensitive technical information that can be used to produce a bioweapon, such as genetic sequence data. Senator Sheldon Whitehouse explained this threat to the Bipartisan Commission on Biodefense in 2015:

> There is a considerable bank of information on biological warfare dating back to the biological warfare planning of the United States and the Soviet Union fifty years ago.... Unlike a nuclear warhead, that information can travel very readily, and in the hands of terrorists or others who wish us harm, it can be very dangerous.[102]

The scope of this security risk is very broad because, worldwide, sensitive pathogen and biodefense information is contained in the computers of governments, industries, and universities.

Failures to collect information early and failures in intelligence. At the onset of the COVID-19 pandemic, information regarding its inception and its progress was poorly disseminated. There was also apparently no prior warning from intelligence services about the looming disaster. Only now, months after the outbreak of the disease, are our intelligence services beginning to get a handle on what happened and when.

All measures to respond to a bioweapons attack are predicated on early detection and quick response. When political considerations interfere with the sharing of information and intelligence services fail to provide warning, any response to an attack is significantly delayed. Every day that goes by in which an attack goes undetected is another day gained from the perspective of a terrorist group. The nation or nations under attack can never regain the time lost.

Delays in decision-making. Most tabletop exercises regarding how to respond to a pandemic or a biological weapons attack cast the participants as having no particular political motives. Data is analyzed and decisions are made based on the clear goal of saving lives. There is but one significant consideration—how best to minimize casualties.

By contrast, the initial responses by nations around the world to the coronavirus pandemic were largely political. China deliberately hid information from other nations, possibly for months. Iran maintained flights to China long past the time it was clear this was almost suicidal because of its desire to maintain its relationship with Beijing. Even President Trump's decision to shut down flights from China ran into an initial blizzard of criticism from domestic opponents more interested in making the president look bad than in saving lives.[103,104]

Shortages of protective gear. For decades, nations and organizations worldwide have talked about the dangers of a pandemic and claimed to have been preparing. Nonetheless, right out of the blocks, even the United States found itself woefully unprepared. There were not enough test kits.[105] There were insufficient stocks of personal protective equipment. Pharmaceuticals were not available. Ventilators had to be rationed.[106]

Worse yet, most of the items that were in short supply had to be manufactured in China and shipped around the world. This meant massive delays. In fighting a virus, time is everything. Running behind means the disease is spreading faster than containment can be implemented, and the result is disaster.

Disease disseminates itself. Much of the science of biological weapons concerns dissemination. Nation-states have spent huge amounts of money attempting to perfect delivery systems and acquire the ability to disseminate biological agents efficiently. The coronavirus spread worldwide in an amazingly short period of time without any known human assistance because it was airborne, easily communicable from one person to another, and spreadable by asymptomatic carriers.

The longer the pandemic continues, the clearer it becomes just how efficiently this virus spreads.[107] We now know that a great many people had the disease and were capable of passing it on to others without knowing they were infected.[108] It is hard to imagine any human-engineered bioweapon delivery system surpassing this level of communicability.

Ease of worldwide spread. Experts have talked for a long time about the way air travel has facilitated the spread of disease. The ongoing pandemic shows just how dramatic this effect can be. An outbreak in a single Chinese city spread in a remarkably short period of time across the entire planet.

It was not only major trunk airline routes that played a role in this. As noted above, the relatively limited but direct air traffic between Iran and China was sufficient to produce an explosion of coronavirus cases in Iran. The continued refusal of Iranian authorities to shut down that conduit for transmission resulted in thousands—if not tens of thousands—of deaths that might have been avoided.

PREDICTIONS: HOW TERRORISTS WILL ADAPT

Considering recent weaknesses and failures of American biodefense during the coronavirus pandemic, it seems reasonable to expect terrorist groups to craft future biological attacks that exploit those weaknesses using the following approaches:

Focus on naturally occurring organisms. It is highly unlikely that any such attack will be built around an engineered organism or an exotic pathogen. It is much more likely that terrorists will choose to use a pathogen that already exists in nature and has been studied.

Acquire organisms from labs. If possible, terrorists will try to steal dangerous pathogens from biolabs. This would allow them to avoid the difficulty and hazards of developing biological agents themselves. The 2020 novel coronavirus showed potential terrorists the type of potential bioweapons that labs around the world have access to and the possibility that a researcher or lab technician in such labs could steal samples of these pathogens.

Terrorists will likely target biolabs outside the United States. Biological research is no longer the province of a handful of research facilities in the United States or Europe—this industry has gone worldwide.[109,110] As a general rule, safeguards will be weaker in biolabs in developing nations that lack the financial and educational resources to properly equip and train laboratory personnel.

Employ simple dissemination from human to human. For a terrorist group looking to choose a pathogen with easy H2H transmissibility, COVID-19 has shown that an airborne pathogen can be spread worldwide without significant assistance.

A handful of members of the terrorist group in question who are willing to act as biological martyrs and allow themselves to be infected could very effectively spread a pathogen bio weapon by frequenting population centers, taking mass transit in crowded cities, and flying on commercial passenger aircraft into key transportation nodes.

To maximize the spread of the disease, these biological martyrs will likely begin their activity on multiple continents simultaneously. They will not light one fire at a time. They will, in effect, light multiple small fires across the globe and allow them to smolder before bursting into flame and attracting attention. This will increase the likelihood that by the time the outbreak has begun to trigger border closures and flight restrictions, it will be too late for any nation to seal itself off.

Get a running start by refraining from announcement until the disease is already a pandemic. A group staging an attack will be highly unlikely to announce they have done so until the disease has already spread across a wide area. The COVID-19 pandemic has highlighted a long series of weaknesses and delays in the response of health officials worldwide. A group seeking maximum impact will not want to spur these officials into rapid, decisive action. It will prefer to allow health officials to bumble along indecisively for as long as possible.

The group launching the attack will acquire the necessary biological agent, infect a certain number of biological martyrs, and turn them loose to spread the disease in crowded subways, concerts, and airport passenger terminals across the planet without making an announcement of any kind. Only when the pandemic has spread worldwide and the window for containment has passed will the group claim credit and fan the flames of worldwide panic by announcing that what is happening is an attack.

IMPLICATIONS: WHAT WE NEED TO DO NOW TO PREPARE

Among the most effective steps we can take to prevent and mitigate a potential bioweapon attack, consider the following:

Know what is out there. We need to know what potential bioweapon pathogens are being worked on and where. We should focus particularly on those pathogens that fit within the methodology outlined above. Which diseases can be easily communicated from human to human, are being widely studied in laboratories, and are accessible to a reasonably competent terrorist group? What are the security and safety procedures in these labs? Where are the weak spots? If we were terrorists looking to buy or steal a bacterium or virus to use in an attack, where would we turn?

Ramp up intelligence. Scientists and physicians like to think of themselves as part of an international fraternity motivated by the pursuit of knowledge and somehow above petty national rivalries. Whatever the truth of that assertion, it does not change the fact that scientists and physicians are still typically subject to the authority of individuals motivated by ideology, patriotism, and the pursuit of partisan advantage.

The Chinese government lied to the world for months about the COVID-19 pandemic. Its scientists and physicians had no capacity to talk past those lies and warn the world. The Chinese Communist Party continues to lie today about this virus. When and if there is another outbreak in China of a deadly disease that threatens humanity, Beijing will lie about that too.

Encouraging cooperation and information sharing is essential. We dare not, though, rely upon the good graces of hostile regimes for our survival. We should have had blanket intelligence coverage of the biolabs in Wuhan and known about any issues in security or safety in real time. We must do whatever is necessary to ensure that we have that kind of coverage of labs from which future pandemics may emanate.

Stockpile—bring key manufacturing home. No matter how good our intelligence, we cannot head off every threat before it materializes. We will need to prepare for another pandemic and stockpile necessary supplies in advance.

We also need to recognize that simply buying and stashing away supplies is insufficient. We must regain the capacity to manufacture our own medical devices, our own protective equipment, and our own pharmaceuticals. The self-destructive drive to offshore production has left us dangerously vulnerable. We must make it a matter of national strategic policy to bring manufacturing home.

Exercise early and often. Having a plan is one thing; being able to implement that plan is quite another. Almost immediately in this crisis we discovered that we were too slow, too hesitant, and too indecisive. The only way to avoid a repetition of this occurrence is to move to a system in which we regularly put our homeland security and emergency response capabilities to the test on a real-world scale.

The terrorists will have most certainly learned their lessons from this pandemic. We must too.

6.

FUTURE BIOWAR: WHAT THE BAD GUYS HAVE LEARNED AND HOW TO COMBAT IT

By Shoshana Bryen and Stephen Bryen

T he idea of biological warfare has been with us over the centuries. With vivid ugliness, Thucydides described the Plague of Athens in 430 BC:

> Strong fevers in the head and a burning redness in the eyes of those who had previously been healthy, and for no apparent reason . . . breathing took on a foul and unpleasant smell . . . pain descended to the chest . . . settled into stomach and caused it to release secretions of bile . . . tiny blisters and ulcers . . . unquenchable thirst . . . progressed to the intestines . . . attacked the genitals.

Mycotoxins, biological agents that can flourish naturally from rotting or spoiled food or grain, would produce that sort of horrible death. Thucydides briefly considered the possibility that the Athenians' enemies had mixed toxin-laden grain in shipments to the Greek imperial capital.

Over the centuries, armies have thrown dead, infected animals over castle walls. The British military chief in North America during the last year of the French and Indian War in 1763 wrote to a trusted colonel, "Could it not be contrived to send smallpox among these disaffected tribes of Indians? We must use every strategem in our power to reduce them."

Japan dropped bio-bombs in World War II, and Saddam Hussein planned to do the same to Israel. The Soviets had an aggressive biological warfare program that it claimed to have shut down, but actually continued and intensified for decades after President Nixon shut down the small U.S. bioweapons program in 1969. Still-unknown perpetrators used the postal service as a delivery system for anthrax to the center of American power in 2001.

THE BAD GUYS

The UN-backed Biological Weapons Convention entered into force in 1975, and most countries in the world signed on. The Convention bans the development, stockpiling, acquisition, retention, and production of biological agents and toxins "of types and in quantities that have no justification for prophylactic, protective, or other peaceful purposes" as well as weapons, equipment, and delivery vehicles "designed to use such agents or toxins for hostile purposes or in armed conflict" and "the transfer of or assistance with acquiring the agents, toxins, weapons, equipment, and delivery vehicles."

Unfortunately, the convention has no inspection or enforcement mechanisms and it is widely believed that many states, like the Soviets did, are conducting bioweapons research and development in secret. Among those known to be doing so are Russia, China, Iran, and North Korea. Russia is a treaty signatory, but even after ratifying the Convention, it supported 18 research centers working on pathogenic bioweapons.

On September 16, 2019, in Novosibirsk, Russia, a gas canister exploded at a reinforced concrete laboratory called the State Research Center of Virology and Biotechnology. The center, formerly the VECTOR facility, is an old Soviet bioweapons lab that now allegedly researches (and houses) Ebola, smallpox, and anthrax—all of which can be used in biowarfare.

Iraq under Saddam used both anthrax and smallpox, among other bio-agents.

Iran got significant help from both China and Russia for its chemical and biological weapons programs despite being a Biological Weapons Convention signatory. The State Department said in an April 2019 report that "Iranian military-controlled facilities, Imam Hossein University (IHU) and Malek Ashtar University (MAU), have researched incapacitating chemical agents." Published Iranian articles have cited weaponizing applications of pharmaceutical-based agents (PBAs), including the powerful opioid fentanyl. The report added that "IHU's chemistry department had sought kilograms of medetomidine—an incapacitating sedative it has researched—from Chinese sellers."

North Korea has an aggressive biological and chemical warfare program, according to the Middlebury Institute of International Studies at Monterey, and is reported to have worked on plague, anthrax, viral hemorrhagic fevers, and smallpox, among other biowar agents, and recruited foreign technicians to help advance its program.

China probably has the most advanced biowarfare program in the world. In 2005, the State Department identified two facilities in China with links to the People's Liberation Army's offensive biological weapons program: the Chinese Ministry of Defense's Academy of Military Medical Sciences (AMMS) Institute of Microbiology and Epidemiology (IME) in Beijing, and the Lanzhou Institute of Biological Products (LIBP). In addition to these two central laboratories, it is estimated that at least 50 other laboratories and hospitals are being used as biological weapons research facilities in China.

China is also advanced in what is called CRISPR-Cas9, a technology that enables geneticists and medical researchers to edit parts of the genome by removing, adding, or altering sections of the DNA sequence. American officials now see CRISPR gene editing as a serious threat to national security. It can lead to precisely targeted bioweapons used to attack a single racial or ethnic group or could be used in combination with vaccines to carry out a biowarfare operation while protecting its own forces. China has also managed to collaborate with most of the world's virologists and geneticists under the cover of peacefully researching viruses and vaccines, no doubt feeding its biowar program.

The FBI has developed cases against Chinese graduate students, at least one of them a PLA officer, at U.S. universities who are part of what appears to be a strategic espionage campaign against American medical and virological research.[111]

There is no consensus on the origins of the COVID-19 pandemic. The Chinese government insists the virus originated in part from horseshoe bats and became zoonotic (anthropozoonotic) , that is, it jumped from bats to humans with some intermediate stop. There is also suspicion that laboratories in Wuhan, and perhaps elsewhere, that were engaged in advanced coronavirus research were the source, and the virus was accidentally leaked from the lab. There is the possibility that the research is actually biological weapons research, though no hard data exists to prove whether or not COVID-19 was a product or byproduct of a weapons program.

WHAT WE KNOW

Some things are clear.

The Chinese government hid the outbreak for months and suppressed information from doctors and nurses on the scene, even repressing the medical professionals themselves. In some cases, experts simply disappeared. In one of the most important early cases, Li Wenliang, a doctor who was severely reprimanded for criticizing the government, was pronounced dead from coronavirus even before he actually died. In other cases, false or misleading information was aired, including the WHO's late-January pronouncement that there was no evidence of H2H transmission of the disease.

To complicate matters, in November 2018, U.S. authorities in Detroit detained a scientist from Wuhan with what the Weapons of Mass Destruction Directorate of the FBI later reported "may be viable Middle East Respiratory Syndrome (MERS) and Severe Acute Respiratory Syndrome (SARS) materials.[112]" A related 2019 investigation in Canada involving a Winnipeg Level 4 lab that researches the most deadly pathogens focused on a researcher who made multiple visits to Wuhan doing "third-party-funded" work in Chinese labs. Canadian authorities deny any link to COVID-19.

While there is no consensus on the origins of COVID-19, there is no doubt that it has been a bonanza for states and terrorists who now know a lot more about critical vulnerabilities of major powers, including the United States and NATO as well as Russia and China:

It is easy for biological toxins, including viruses, to spread rapidly and broadly, even on a global scale.

Manufacturing and supply-chain distribution systems crucial to the economy and public health are extremely vulnerable to disruption.

First responder and hospital systems lack surge capacity and can be overwhelmed.

It is easy to create shortages of medical supplies, from the simplest equipment that was once considered commodities to more complex products such as ventilators and pharmacological supplies.

A virus can delay, repurpose, or simply halt military operations, enabling an adversary like China to take advantage.

Economic activity is severely reduced and markets in capitalist countries become stressed, losing value to depression levels.

Producing detection systems, vaccines, and effective treatments is time-consuming and uncertain, with distribution of such solutions adding to logistical burdens and social anxiety.

Response measures can, over weeks, "flatten the curve" of infection to avoid overwhelming medical facilities, but cannot stop the spread of infection and can lead to a false sense of security.

Irresponsible news media and politicians can spread unrest and panic, undermining trust in a government's ability to cope with a biowar crisis.

Hostile states use disinformation, denial, and deception to hide responsibility while at the same time seeking significant political, economic, and military advantages in the midst of a crisis.

STRATEGIES FOR THE FUTURE

While many experts focused on the coronavirus lockdown and its eventual lifting, less attention was given to the degradation of the U.S. military and weakening of America's strategic deterrence, especially in East Asia.

Concomitant with a loss of deterrence is a rise in the risk of general war, especially with the Chinese Communist Party becoming more militant as it shed its image as a benign power to become more nationalistic and jingoistic.

There are two keys to preparing for a future biological disaster: a strategy that keeps the military and critical industries operating and far better intelligence on "bad" actors, especially Russia and China. Both the strategy and intelligence need massive improvement.

Neither the U.S. Navy nor the Pentagon at large were prepared for a pandemic. Their decisions resulted in the withdrawal of the aircraft carrier USS *Theodore Roosevelt* and its battle group from the region. In early March 2020, the Navy persisted in "normal" port calls to areas with rising coronavirus infection rates—the *Roosevelt* went to Vietnam and the crew was on the ground for 5 days. Ships were then "quarantined" at sea for 14 days. The Navy had to know by then that the quarantine of cruise ship passengers and crew together at sea meant the virus would spread widely among those on board. At the same time, while the Pentagon canceled all travel, military exercises, and deployments, it did not countermand the Navy's decision to "quarantine" 5,000 people together. Crew among the USS *Ronald Reagan* battle group also became infected, raising the brief possibility of the disabling of all major U.S. naval surface vessels in the Indo-Pacific region.

Beijing took advantage of the absence of the *Roosevelt* by stepping up operations in the South China Sea and sending 5,000 troops into a contested border region with India, leading to concerns that Chinese Communist military leaders may push for action against other targets, including Taiwan.

The Pentagon and military services must find a better way to secure effective fighting forces under pandemic conditions. Part of the answer would seem to be in pre-positioning testing kits, protective masks, and decontamination equipment in safe zones located on or near important U.S. military bases. Clearly the Pentagon has been scrambling for answers, including having many of its personnel telework, which created extreme new security problems for American defenses. The situation for military personnel and dependents abroad should be a top priority.

The United States needs a strategy to secure its critical industries. If specialized plants reduce output or cease working altogether, the damage to our capabilities could be enormous. A civil strategy to keep businesses, including small businesses, operating would significantly reduce the need for damaging and often counterproductive lockdown or quarantine measures.

During the Gulf War and Iraq War, Israel set an important civil defense example by providing kits to all its citizens that included gas masks and antibiotics to be used in case of a biological attack. The distribution of kits ended in 2014, but what Israel did stands as an excellent example of what the United States and other nations could do to protect against pandemics caused by viruses. A properly designed kit for every citizen (Israel had baby kits and kits adjusting for long beards) would go a long way to protect lives and keep the country working, meaning that lockdowns and other measures could be confined to hot spot locations and only when absolutely needed.

Kits might include high-quality face masks, synthetic rubber gloves, and, most importantly, general purpose antiviral compounds. The last is not yet available but their development would help reduce fear in the public, stop hoarding practices that harm social trust, and keep transportation systems operating. It would also reduce pressure on doctors, nurses, and hospitals.

Another critical need is vastly improved intelligence so that dangers can be anticipated, avoided, or mitigated. A great deal is known about China's biological research operations because of extensive contacts and cooperation between Chinese and foreign scientists, and projects shared among Chinese, American, French, Australian, and other laboratories. For a brief three years (2014–2017), the United States recognized the risk in certain types of viral research and urged scientists to cease, going so far as to halt funding from the National Institutes of Health and other organizations. But in 2017 the ban was dropped.

Our scientific establishment returned to business as usual with no real strategic assessment of the risks involved, although there were warnings. The FBI was concerned about biological agents, including SARs viruses, being moved in and out of the United States, and U.S. Customs seized some of this material. Likewise, the CIA evidenced serious concern about certain biological warfare dangers, particularly from terrorists. But available information does not reassure us that anyone in our intelligence system has systematically dug into what China was doing.

SPECIFIC STEPS

The United States needs a broad range of specific changes and improvements to U.S. management of proactive responses to biothreats, including the following:

1. Suspend U.S.-sponsored biological research with China for Class A Bioterrorism Agents, which are defined as "organisms that pose a risk to national security." Such agents can easily be disseminated or transmitted from person to person, can result in high

mortality rates, have the potential for major public health impact, might cause public panic and social disruption, and could require special action for public health preparedness.

2. Expand the CDC Class A Bioterrorism Agents and Diseases list to include all coronavirus types without exception, including coronavirus variants and mutations, and experimentation in zoonotic (anthropozoonotic) transfer of virus agents, variations, and mutations.

3. Strongly urge American scientists not to cooperate in any Class A Bioterrorism Agent research with Chinese counterparts and withhold U.S. government funding to them and their institutions if they do so.

4. Cancel visas to Chinese researchers who are in the United States or are coming to the United States to work on Class A Bioterrorism Agents.

5. Require compensation from the Chinese Communist Party for the coronavirus epidemic and use the International Court of Justice to bring a case against the Chinese regime.*

6. Demand a credible and independent WHO inspection of China's virology laboratories.

7. Demand that Taiwan be included in the WHO as a condition of any future U.S. funding of the WHO.

8. Strengthen U.S. defenses in the Pacific, including Guam, Japan, and Okinawa. Instead of withdrawing

---

* While the likelihood of #5 and #6 are minimal and American leverage is weak, the point is to clearly state the American position and perhaps encourage countries whose experience with COVID-19 inclines them toward a full accounting to take a stand with Washington. As an alternative to #7, the U.S. should consider a "democracies group" including Taiwan, Israel, NATO countries, and U.S. allies in Asia and Latin America.

U.S. bomber forces from Guam, the United States should bolster the force there and add air defenses to protect both the airfields and the harbor used by the U.S. Navy.

9. Consider basing sophisticated air defense systems in Taiwan (perhaps using Israel's Arrow III system, which is available now), run by the U.S. in partnership with Taiwan.

10. Work with Japan to move quickly to strengthen its air defense systems, especially around ports and harbors, and to restore the recently canceled missile defense sites in Akita Prefecture, planned to host two AEGIS Ashore missile defense bases capable of operating Standard Missile 3 Block IIA interceptor missiles as well as Standard Missile 6 interceptors.

CONCLUSION

As the world emerges from the pandemic, major flaws in the "Chinese model" have appeared: numerous countries have junked defective coronavirus test kits from China, while others have recalled tens of thousands of defective Chinese-origin N-95 face masks. Countries in China's Belt and Road Initiative are complaining about the heavy economic burden of mandatory Chinese "loans." If China is not reaping the benefits it sought to claim during the early confusion of the West, an opportunity for the United States to reassert leadership may appear. The country must be ready to step up.

7.

UNDERSTANDING THE BIOWEAPONS THREAT AND ITS IMPLICATIONS FOR DEFENSE AGAINST NATURAL EPIDEMICS

By Ken Alibek and Albina Tskhay

INTRODUCTION

The understanding that microorganisms can be used for more than food, beer, and wine has led not only to the initial interest in biological weapons (BW), but eventually to the beginning of concrete work on the creation of biological weapons. Of the three types of weapons of mass destruction, biological weapons are the first in the history of creation, and for a long time, they were considered weapons of mass destruction. In fact, biological weapons are mass casualty weapons since they infect, afflict, and kill the human population but do not destroy infrastructure.

These weapons have been considered attractive as a means of conducting wars; the first attempts to design and test some modern

Official Soviet Army photo of Ken Alibek, taken in 1982 after he was promoted to deputy director of Omutninsk. He was wearing a medal for "wartime services" awarded for the successful development of a tularemia biological weapon.

types were undertaken at the beginning of the 20th century. In fact, the idea first came to scientists after the epidemic of pulmonary plague in Manchuria and Transbaikalia (1910-1911). In the 1920s, the Soviet Bolshevik government decided to develop a large and relatively sophisticated biological weapons program. Soon thereafter, it began BW research and development, accumulating more and more knowledge in the field of biological warfare.

Over a period of 70 years, this has resulted in production methods, delivery and application methods, and a specific strategy for performing BW attacks. The knowledge that was accumulated during this period showed that despite several possible methods of using BW, the most effective is the creation of aerosols of non-contagious and contagious biological agents such as viruses and bacteria. However, combat formulations based on contagious infectious agents were developed to create large-scale epidemics. In particular, for a long time, plague and smallpox (Variola major) were prioritized as strategic variants of biological weapons. Their potential to cause enormous epidemics with many secondary, tertiary, and further infections would result in a huge number of human casualties, disruption of normal life, destruction of economic potential, and, ultimately even a complete collapse in the country where the attack took place.

With the understanding that epidemics caused by biological aerosols as a result of BW attacks and natural outbreaks have some similarities and differences, this chapter is dedicated to describing an outbreak caused by deployment of a BW and comparing it to natural outbreaks. Based on this, we discuss a possible concept and means to develop appropriate anti-epidemic, prophylactic, and therapeutic measures.

PART I: THE HISTORY OF BW

Modern history. Throughout the history of humankind, there have been many attempts to use infections as a means of biological warfare. However, until the beginning of the 20th century, the level of sophistication was low, and the use of ancient methods is not applicable for discussing modern BW methods of deployment. Below we mention some programs that were significant and whose existence is openly described.

After the Russian Revolution in 1917, Soviet Bolsheviks decided to expand BW efforts and intensified research in the fields of BW. Their first attempts to make BW on a large scale and test them were in 1923 on the Solovetsky Islands. The work on different types of BW continued until the early 1990s, when President Mikhail Gorbachev signed a top-secret decree to terminate a large portion of the Soviet programs. Throughout the program's existence, many types of biological weapons were developed and tested. Among them were anthrax, plague, tularemia, Q-fever, glanders, melioidosis, smallpox, and Venezuelan equine encephalomyelitis, representing bacterial, rickettsial, and viral biological weapons. Ebola and Marburg hemorrhagic fever were developed at later stages. Throughout the program's existence, different methods for deploying BW were studied, and the final conclusion was that the most sophisticated method of deployment would be aerosol dissemination.

Another BW program, starting in the 1940s, was established by the United States. It continued through three decades until 1972, when President Nixon signed a presidential order to terminate both the bacterial/viral and toxin biological weapons programs. The program was mostly focused on bacterial agents like *B. anthracis* (anthrax), Staphylococcal enterotoxin B, tularemia, and Venezuelan equine encephalomyelitis. Some small initial studies on smallpox were conducted before the 1970s. The size of the program was much smaller compared to the biggest one established by the Soviet Union. But even in this case, some information was collected resulting from several research projects, production attempts, and field trials.

The United States program focused mostly on noncontagious agents and was based on the principle of not developing biological weapons for which there was no cure or prevention. Therefore, there was no significant accumulation of knowledge to understand the peculiarities of epidemic development when deploying infectious agents capable of causing highly contagious, unpreventable, and incurable diseases.

Another relatively large program had been established by the Japanese military and mostly focused on bacterial agents, including plague and anthrax. Little information was retrieved from the program by the Soviet military, who captured some documentation and personnel in August–September 1945. The major knowledge acquired was how to make large amounts of bacterial agents and how to deploy them using certain types of unsophisticated bombs.

A more contemporary biological weapons program was established by South Africa, but it was more of a terrorist/diversionary type of program. Here, there was not enough information about large-scale deployment of these weapons over large territories.

In addition to these known programs, relatively small biological weapons programs were established by Saddam Hussein in Iraq, but it is important to note that this program existed only until 1991, when it was dismantled after several visits from American inspectors. The latest information about BW programs in Iraq was obtained in 1995. This information was fragmentary and lacked information about field tests, meaning that there was no information about epidemic development as a result of the Iraqi program.

It is also known that some countries, like the United Kingdom, Germany, and Czechoslovakia, had some relatively limited BW programs. Other countries, like China, North Korea, and Iran, are still suspected of having clandestine military-type BW programs. Possible regularities of epidemics caused by the deployment of contagious BW have been studied within the Soviet Union's offensive BW program. Although a variety of pathogen deployment methods have been studied, research of smallpox epidemics shows epidemic patterns similar to those of the current COVID-19 pandemic. Proceeding from this, we will focus on the analysis of smallpox epidemic prediction and compare it with COVID-19.

SMALLPOX: INFECTION AND PROGNOSTIC EPIDEMICS

One of the most deadly and contagious BWs ever developed is smallpox. Smallpox affects people of all ages but has the highest mortality rates among the young and the elderly. Transmission primarily occurs via the respiratory route (from nasal and oral secretions) and infection can occur with as little as ten viral particles. The mortality rate of naturally occurring cases in untreated individuals is between 20% and 50%. Death usually results from viremia, toxemia, disseminated intravascular coagulation, hypotension, or cardiovascular collapse.

There are three phases of clinical manifestation of traditional smallpox infection: incubation, which usually lasts between 7 and 14 days (with a range of 4 to 19 days), prodrome, and pox/manifestation period. The prodromal period is characterized by a high fever (38.5 °C to 40.5 °C) and other symptoms including malaise, headache, and backache. The period of manifestation begins when small, red lesions appear on the patient's tongue and palate. The telltale rash also appears during the final phase. The rash first appears in the form of macules that progress to papules, then to vesicles, which turn into scabs that gradually fall off, leaving unpigmented marks. Individuals are contagious until all of the scabs have fallen off. The differential diagnosis includes monkeypox and chickenpox. Distinguishable features of a smallpox rash are a centrifugal distribution of lesions that tend to appear monomorphic (all one stage) and are deep-seated, firm to the touch, and round, with a common appearance on the soles of the feet and palms of the hands. There are two less common but more severe forms of smallpox infection, the flat and hemorrhagic forms. There is no specific treatment for smallpox disease and the only prevention is vaccination.

Potential methods of release and consequences of smallpox attack. A biological attack using smallpox could be conducted in several ways:

- by contaminating various articles and food,
- by dispatching an intentionally infected terrorist,
- by using mechanical devices to generate an aerosol in the open air or an enclosed space, or
- by incorporating the pathogen in an explosive device.

Explosion and spraying are by far the most efficient and effective modes of deploying biological weapons. Aerosol dispersion is the only method that can effectively be used against large target areas. Practically any biological threat agent can cause a pulmonary infection, and such infections are often more severe and more lethal than the naturally occurring form of the infection. Thus, an effective biological defense must first and foremost involve protection against an aerosol attack.

In military scenarios, the use of aerosolized biological weapons and the methods used to deploy them are usually designed to provide devastating effects over large areas. Although Soviet military planning determined that non-contagious biological weapons can be deployed, for example, using a medium-range bomber equipped with two 2-ton spray tanks that could effectively cover more than 1,000 km² of territory, contagious agents like smallpox were considered strategic weapons and deployed very deep into the territory of an enemy country. Proceeding from this, contagious biological weapons like smallpox would only be deployed using single- or multi-warhead operational or strategic missiles. However, even a small-scale military or terrorist attack could cause a significant number of casualties, as well as tremendous panic and disruption of the economy and other vital activities.

Understanding contagiousness, route of infection, and type of infection would give comprehension of prospective damage caused by smallpox, which is capable of producing a large number of casualties in the first wave of infected people and later an epidemic spread resulting from the appearance of the secondary and further infected population.

Testing a smallpox biological weapon and its potential effectiveness. Prior to the late 1970s, field testing of smallpox biological weapons in the Soviet Union was conducted at Rebirth Island in the Aral Sea. Field testing was halted in the late 1970s because of the potential of creating an epidemic after naturally occurring smallpox had been eradicated, and because the Soviet Union had signed the 1972 Biological Weapons Convention.

Though field testing of the smallpox weapon was halted, other forms of testing continued. In the late 1980s, new variants of the smallpox weapon (those produced using large-scale fermentation in 250 L or 630 L reactors) were tested using exploding micromodels of bomblets loaded with a smallpox formulation in small chambers. Using mathematical modeling, the results were then extrapolated to determine the effects that would be seen if used as a full-scale weapon. In December of 1990, testing of the new large-scale reactor formulation was completed and all necessary calculations to determine the possible effectiveness of a new smallpox weapon were evaluated.

Since smallpox biological weapons have never been used on a large scale such as that envisioned by the Soviets, no data were available on the actual danger and expected losses encountered with these weapons. However, using what was known about smallpox, it was possible to estimate the potential damage. Drawing from the knowledge of smallpox as a disease, Soviet experts concluded that the effectiveness of smallpox biological weapons would depend on the following characteristics:

- the infectious dose (LD_{50} is only 10–20 viral particles);

- its stability in an aerosol and its ability to travel for many miles without the loss of virulence (the liquid formulation of smallpox is stable in an aerosol and remains viable for many miles);

- its ability to survive in the environment for days or even weeks (smallpox is capable of this);

- the number of vaccinated civilians or troops (smallpox vaccination is no longer required for these groups);

- its index of contagiousness (the index of contagiousness for smallpox is from 0.6 to 0.9 [number of diseased/number of contacts]);

- the length of the incubation period (the incubation period for smallpox is relatively short at 7–17 days, the use of smallpox in a weaponized aerosol form will likely shorten this period, and the first cases can be expected to appear by day 3 or 4 after infection);

- the length of time people remain infectious (people infected with smallpox could already be contagious in the prodromal period, before they have specific signs of disease, and remain contagious throughout the course of the disease);

- the length of time corpses remain infectious (though irrelevant under regular circumstances, in the event of a massive aerosol attack with a high number of casualties, corpses of smallpox fatalities will remain infectious for a long time—days to months, depending primarily on environmental temperature); and

- the severity of the clinical picture (with smallpox infection, the clinical picture is extremely severe in many cases).

PART II. IMPLICATION OF BW COUNTERMEASURES FOR DEFENSE AGAINST NATURAL EPIDEMICS

COVID-19: A scenario of natural epidemic in modernity. As of May 19, 2020, the COVID-19 pandemic resulted in the following consequences:

- Over 92,000 people died (fatality rate is more than 6%).
- Over 30 million people lost their jobs.
- Many industries were disrupted or nearly destroyed.
- Thousands of large and small companies went bankrupt.
- Domestic violence increased (many do not withstand months indoors).
- Curricula at universities and schools were disrupted.
- People were buried in mass graves.

There have been heated debates about whether this pandemic was manmade or natural. In order to answer this, we should analyze the following:

- The infectious dose of SARS-CoV-2 has not been determined, but it is very likely to be very low (a few to several viral particles).
- Its stability in an aerosol and its ability to travel for many miles without the loss of virulence are low
- Its ability to survive in the environment is moderate (few hours)
- The number of vaccinated civilians or troops is nil
- Its contagiousness is high (not precisely defined but comparable or maybe higher than smallpox)
- The length of the incubation period is still not precisely known (average is 2 to 14 days and up to 28 days).
- The length of time people remain infectious is long (people infected with COVID-19 could already be contagious 1 to 2 days prior to showing symptoms, before they have specific signs of disease, and remain contagious throughout the course of the disease).
- The corpses of the deceased remain infectious for a long time.

- The severity of the clinical picture varies (high for certain population groups and mild for healthy and young individuals).
- The number of infected people appearing at the beginning of the epidemic was low, with exponential growth over time.

As it is seen, there are still many unknowns when it comes to making certain conclusions, but the following description shows how the pandemic developed over time. However, it is important to mention that due to the incomplete openness of the Chinese government, there is no full picture of pandemic development and the figures revealed could involve some approximation.

As it is known today, the first documented case, which was identified by analyzing disease history and testing samples, is dated November 17, 2019. According to Chinese government data, this was a 55-year old patient from Hubei Province. Every day since that date, anywhere from one to five new cases were registered. By December 15, 2019, the number of infected reached 27, and in 5 days, by December 20, the number of confirmed cases reached 60.

A significant number of infected patients were registered at the end of December. On December 27, more than 180 people were infected, later reaching 266 by December 31 and 381 by the first day of the new year.

Attempts to identify "patient zero" have not been a success. Practically all people infected by then were 39 to 79 years old. At that point it was already possible that some of the infected were secondary patients, i.e., that the infection was transmittable from person to person. On January 9, 2020, the Chinese government announced that the cause of the new epidemic was a new coronavirus, later named SARS-CoV-2 (severe acute respiratory syndrome coronavirus 2).

On January 11, some Chinese health authorities claimed that at that time there were only 41 confirmed cases of the disease. But based on the fact that in just one day (December 31, 2019–January 1, 2020), the detected number of infected and sick people had increased by more than 100 people, it is likely that the actual number of people infected on that date was significantly higher, possibly reaching more than 1000 people.

Further, a significant mistake was made by the health officials who declared a quarantine only on January 23 and only in Wuhan Province. Moreover, although official information from China stated that on

January 22 there were only 570 cases of infection in the country, the real number was significantly higher, very likely at least 10,000 cases. By January 20, it was evident that the outbreak had begun taking the form of an epidemic because the alleged first case outside of China appeared on January 20 in Thailand.

Some additional information showed that, by then, Chinese health officials were aware of the onset of the disease:

- They were aware of the first patient, who unequivocally indicated that this was a new infection, on December 12, 2019, since the number of cases known to them at that time was at least 59 and patient examination showed that this was a new infection caused by unknown virus.

- On December 27, 2019, a patient was admitted to a hospital in France with a disease that was undiagnosed at that time, but later, with a retrospective analysis, it turned out that he had COVID-19 (this patient, however, did not travel to China).

- Later, by retrospective analysis, 14 more patients were identified in France, dating back to December 2019.

It is very likely that the quarantine measures taken by China on January 23, 2020, should have been taken no later than mid-December 2019 and probably would have prevented the pandemic. The fact that this infection had already begun to spread around the world, not on January 20 as it was officially supposed, but in December 2019, was critical to helping establish the pandemic's proportions.

The pattern of infection shows that there was no BW attack, but it was a natural epidemic with a new coronavirus.

SMALLPOX AND COVID-19 COMPARISON

In the case of relatively limited application, it is unlikely that a smallpox attack would result in a super-catastrophic event with the loss of many millions of lives. At the same time, however, underestimating the possible consequences of an attack would be a dangerous and costly mistake. An attack using smallpox formulations in any form will result in tremendous cost in terms of loss of life and psychological and economical damage to the country where the attack occurs.

A BW attack may go undetected until victims begin to fall ill, which will complicate diagnosis, treatment, and containment efforts. Once a biological attack has been detected, additional time will likely pass before the causative agent has been conclusively identified, again complicating diagnosis, treatment, and containment efforts. It will be difficult to determine the size and perimeter of the contaminated areas, in turn making it difficult to estimate the number of exposed, identify those exposed, and determine where to conduct decontamination operations if necessary. The target population is not likely to be vaccinated against the threat agent. The smallpox vaccines that exist, even with immediate application, will be helpful only in a matter of time since they do not reach full effectiveness until days to weeks after inoculation. The treatment regimen for smallpox is complex and the duration of the disease is long, requiring the efforts of a large number of medical and support personnel. Even in the case of a relatively small amount released, initially there could be hundreds or even thousands of casualties. Victims would need to be isolated and treated as soon as possible after exposure. However, the large number of patients would make it impossible to successfully treat them all; existing medical and support personnel, medications, and medical equipment would not be sufficient. Depending on the size of the aerosol attack, the number of casualties may initially vary from a relatively small number to many thousands.

As the epidemic progresses, new factors would direct its course: secondary droplet infections, which are caused by the virus being excreted into bodily fluids and then aerosolized (by a cough or a sneeze, for example), and secondary non-aerosol infections, which in the case of smallpox would primarily be caused by contact with the live virus on contaminated surfaces and in human cadavers. With smallpox, secondary droplet infections would be of great significance because of smallpox's high degree of contagiousness. Although smallpox is not as contagious as other diseases that are nearly absolutely contagious, such as measles, a very significant number of people would become secondarily infected.

Since this chapter is being written in mid-May of 2020, not much is known about SARS-CoV-2. The information provided has some limitations. However, it is sufficient at this point to show similarities and differences, which are outlined below.

- Both Variola major and SARS-CoV-2 are transmitted from person to person.
- Variola major is an anthroponotic (a disease transmitted from humans to animals) virus; SARS-CoV-2 is anthropozoonotic (a disease transmitted from animals to humans).
- Both viruses are enveloped,[113] while variola is a DNA virus and SARS-CoV-2 is an RNA virus.
- Variola is one of the largest viruses. while SARS-CoV-2 is a relatively simple RNA virus.
- The infectious dose for both is very low.
- The major route of infection is the respiratory tract for both.
- The contact route of infection is an additional factor in infection for both.
- Variola major is more stable than SARS-CoV-2.
- Both viruses multiply initially in the respiratory tract.
- The incubation period is similar for both (for smallpox, it is 4 to 14 days; for COVID-19, it is 2 to 14 days).
- Patients are contagious in the late incubation period or in the early prodromal period when infected with both viruses.

Similarities and differences in clinical manifestations. The following is a comparison of the clinical features of smallpox and COVID-19.

- While smallpox is a pantropic (virus that can invade and affect many different tissues of the body) systemic infection with severe viral dissemination and systemic effects in skin and mucosal membranes, COVID-19 is mainly a pulmonary disease, damaging alveoli and blocking lung microcirculation, producing septicemia, and resulting in oxygen deprivation to organs and tissues.
- Smallpox has three distinct forms: ordinary, hemorrhagic, and flat. COVID-19 is mainly a disease, the clinical manifestations of which are a result of acute respiratory distress syndrome.

- Mortality for the unvaccinated is 30–50% for the ordinary smallpox form and 90–100% for the flat and hemorrhagic smallpox forms. COVID-19 has low mortality, not exceeding 3-4%.

- Smallpox is equally infectious and lethal for all ages, while COVID-19 is a disease of the immunocompromised, elderly, and otherwise diseased, and those with chronic conditions.

Epidemiology. The following compares the incidence, distribution, and control of smallpox and COVID-19.

- In the case of smallpox deployed as a biological weapon, the number of casualties appearing simultaneously or almost simultaneously is very high. In the case of COVID-19, single or limited cases of infection began to appear, followed by an accumulation of new cases over time.

- A smallpox BW attack will cause very large foci of infection to form, with immediate overwhelm of the entire medical care system in the area of application. COVID-19 is less catastrophic; if the medical system is not overwhelmed at the beginning of the epidemic, after new cases accumulate, the number of medical personnel will increase without causing severe devastation because there will be more time to prepare for the epidemic.

- Smallpox infection would produce new cases only by transmission from person to person. With COVID-19, one more transmission mechanism should not be forgotten: human-to-animal and animal-to-human.

- It will be much more difficult to contain a smallpox epidemic because panicking people will flow into medical facilities for treatment, further infecting new people while demanding assistance. In the case of COVID-19, more effective measures can be introduced since it is possible to involve more people for containment—COVID-19 does not require any specific treatment for younger people and for those whose disease is mild. Anti-epidemic and therapeutic measures should be focused on specific populations.

- In the case of a smallpox BW weapon attack, the appearance of large numbers of infected and deceased people will produce an enormous challenge to healthcare facilities and medical personnel. Smallpox infection, due to its severity, will require a significant number of personnel to treat even a single patient. In the case of COVID-19, treatment is still challenging but the current understanding is that the major focus should be on patients with chronic conditions, those who are overweight and obese, and those who are over 50 years old. While still a significant challenge, the burden of effort would be lower than in the case of smallpox infection.

- Another big challenge and threat is the ability of Variola major to infect medical personnel of any age and produce a high mortality rate among physicians and nurses. In the case of COVID-19, younger medical workers have a lower chance of developing a lethal infection, and application of an age requirement for members of medical teams would reduce the number of fatalities among medical personnel.

- One of the most difficult problems in the case of both infections is the large number of dead. In both cases, it would be necessary to have a significant number of coffins of special design, appropriate disinfectants, and specific locations for burying the thousands of cases occurring within short periods of time. But in the case of smallpox, this situation would be more complicated due to the high rate of infection, high level of infectiousness, and high mortality rate.

Thus, with the smallpox biological weapon, the number of casualties would differ considerably from that seen with the use of SARS-CoV-2. For SARS-CoV-2, the number of new cases would build up to a peak and then plateau for an indefinite time, until all employed anti-epidemic measures become effective. With smallpox, the number of new cases would build up to a peak between the 3rd and 17th day after deployment and then plateau. In both cases, a new peak formed by secondary cases would appear and would then be followed by a new plateau, etc. At some point, due to implementation of appropriate anti-epidemic measures, the number of cases would stabilize, forming a long-lasting plateau that would finally start subsiding, either disappearing completely or having a long-lasting tail in the form of single or small-group cases.

The duration of these plateaus and peaks would depend on the intensity of the secondary infections, primarily the secondary droplet infections. The length of time it would take to reach a reduction in the number of cases depends on

- the number of people infected by the primary aerosols (in the case of smallpox);

- the number of people infected before the initial anti-epidemic measures are implemented;

- the transportation of people from the site of the original attack in the first hours and days after the attack or natural epidemic initiation, as they can form new epidemic foci (for both smallpox and COVID-19);

- the effectiveness of quarantine, isolation, disinfection, and cadaver disposal measures (for both smallpox and COVID-19); and

- the intensity and effectiveness of treatment and emergency prophylactic (vaccination) and other measures (for both smallpox and COVID-19).

However, a smallpox biological weapons attack and a natural epidemic caused by SARS-CoV-2 would have ramifications other than just human casualties:

- a complete or partial disruption of vital (including business, travel, production, tourism, and others) activity for a relatively long period of time;

- an extreme shortage of medical and auxiliary personnel to stop the epidemic and reduce its consequences;

- a lack of adequate pharmaceutical and medical preparations and supplies for treatment, emergency prophylaxis, and infection prevention;

- the disruption of normal life activities, severe disruption of businesses, and economic crisis due to panic in the case of a smallpox attack.

Thus, the potential results of a biological weapons attack caused by contagious viruses like SARS-CoV-2 are large numbers of diseased and dead, a panicked populace, an overwhelmed health care system, and dramatic disruption of economic and vital activities. Additionally, in the case of a smallpox BW attack, the number of casualties will be dramatically larger.

CONCLUSION

The continuously growing threat of natural epidemics caused by newly emerging viruses makes understanding the threat and the types of medical defense needed to address it critical. A more comprehensive understanding of this emerging threat, based on our knowledge of the threat posed by bioterrorism, will direct us to the appropriate avenues to address this threat and will result in novel prophylactic and therapeutic methods and means for diseases caused by both biological weapons and natural epidemics.

8.

How Can We Develop Reliable Defense in an Uncertain World?

By Ken Alibek and Albina Tskhay

As generals fight not a new but a previous war, in the field of epidemic defense, we do the same.

Infectious diseases have always been a threat to humanity, causing a large number of deaths, and until the last century they were the main cause of death. Over time, methods of prevention and treatment were developed and now include disinfectants, vaccines, antibiotics, antivirals, monoclonal antibodies, and more. However, the emergence of new infectious agents, natural mutations, and manmade manipulations used to create bioweapons still make infectious diseases a danger.

Although humanity has faced numerous outbreaks, epidemics, and pandemics caused by various bacterial and viral diseases throughout the course of history, the measures taken to protect the population have not change significantly. During the Spanish Flu pandemic in 1918, the main prophylactic measures were the same as those we see in 2020—self-isolation, quarantine, and face masks—despite the substantial progress humanity has made in the science of infectious diseases and medicine.

Today's COVID-19 pandemic shows that no country is prepared to face the threat of infectious disease regardless of whether the source of infection is nature or the laboratory. In this regard, this chapter will consider currently available, used, and forgotten prophylaxes and treatments to raise the question of preparedness for future threats.

Manmade vs. Natural Epidemics

There are several tools to distinguish between natural and manmade epidemics, for instance, the Grunow-Finke Assessment Tool, the modified Grunow-Finke Assessment Tool, the Bioterrorism Risk

Assessment (BTRA), and others. The purpose of these tools is to assess a disease's characteristics and, based on the overall score, to determine the type of epidemic or pandemic.

Below, for example, are criteria for distinguishing between natural and manmade epidemics using the Grunow-Finke Assessment Tool. Each parameter is assigned a certain score (0, No data; 1, Uncertain; 2, Obvious peculiarities; 3, Clear indication or proof of a biological attack) and if the resulting overall score is <50%, it is concluded that the case is a natural outbreak; if the score is >50%, it is most likely an unnatural outbreak. The criteria assessed are as follows:

- bio-risk
- biothreat
- peculiarities of the intensity and dynamics of the epidemic
- peculiarities of the transmission mode of the biological agent
- peculiarities of the time of the epidemic
- unusually rapid spread of the epidemic
- limitation of the epidemic to a specific population
- peculiarities of the clinical manifestation
- special aspects of the biological agent
- peculiarities of the geographic distribution of the biological agent
- high concentration of the biological agent in the environment
- identification of the agent as a biological warfare agent
- proof of the release of the agent by a biological weapon

Based on the answers to these questions, it can be deduced that manmade epidemics are more difficult to prevent and control due to artificially enhanced virulence factors, contagiousness, and infectivity. So, speaking in the context of manmade epidemics, protective measures should be scrupulously designed to ensure universal anti-infectious defense. At the same time, such well-developed and properly applied prophylactic safeguards will provide protection against natural epidemics.

VACCINATION AS A MEANS OF DEFENSE

Vaccines have become a very effective tool of protection against infectious diseases. Today, vaccines save about 2.5 million lives annually, which is more than any therapeutic method existing. However, *most* vaccines are only applicable for known pathogens. Examples of vaccines that have already been developed (and some licensed) include botulism, anthrax, plague, tularemia, Q-fever, viral hemorrhagic fever, smallpox, and typhoid fever. These vaccines are an effective means of prophylaxis and may ensure a high level of population protection, not only because of individual adaptive immunity but also as a result of acquired herd immunity. These vaccines are also effective against antibiotic- and antiviral-resistant pathogen strains. They have already been developed and stockpiled and there is no need to conduct safety and pharmacodynamics studies because these have already been conducted.

However, it is not possible to rely solely on vaccines to ensure biosafety against natural and manmade outbreaks and epidemics. In the case of newly emerging infectious diseases, vaccines aiming to ensure the acquisition of adaptive immunity are probably not the most sophisticated method of protection since it usually takes about 8 to 10 years on average to develop, test, and license a vaccine. On the other hand, it may take only 1 to 3 years to develop a new type of biological weapon.

It is obvious that it is not feasible for bioterrorists to use biological weapons against which effective vaccines have been developed and stockpiled. But using methods of molecular biology, it is possible to change the antigens of a pathogen to make even available vaccines ineffective. Apart from this, some live-attenuated vaccines can cause serious side effects and complications in immunocompromised and aged individuals, who are often at highest risk to become infected and deceased due to an infection. Moreover, even when vaccines are available, it will still take a certain period of time to protect the population after an attack happens. Since for some infectious agents the incubation period may last days or even weeks, vaccine administration may be too late to avoid serious consequences and high mortality.

CURRENT MEDICAL DEFENSE AGAINST BIOLOGICAL WEAPONS AND NATURAL EPIDEMICS

Another defense against biological weapons is post-exposure treatment with antibiotics and antivirals. These can be applied to victims of biological weapons who are proven or suspected to be exposed to the infectious agent, saving a lot of lives. However, currently, the market of broad-spectrum antibiotics and antivirals is very small, while the creation of a resistant pathogen strain can make the existing treatment options ineffective. The situation with COVID-19 has shown that available antivirals are not effective enough and may cause serious and even fatal side effects. For instance, the anti-malarial medication chloroquine was not previously studied for conditions like coronavirus or other viral infections, and therefore its administration resulted in an increased rate of cardiovascular system-related fatalities. The difficulty with creating a "library" of pharmaceuticals against biological weapon threats is based on the fact that there are hundreds of microorganisms that can potentially be used as weapons. Thus, it is usually resource-consuming and time-extensive to develop effective chemotherapeutics against these threats, while some will even appear to be unnecessary.

DYNAMIC VS. PATHOGEN-SPECIFIC PROTECTION

Based on the peculiarities of the methods we currently rely on, pathogen-specific protection measures are not an adequate choice. Recently, the COVID-19 pandemic has shown that we are unprepared for unexpected biological threats. On the other hand, apart from pathogen-specific protection approaches, another potential defense is based on enhancing the population's immunity to make it less susceptible and vulnerable to infectious agents. Although this approach will not likely give 100% protection, especially against highly deadly pathogens, it will nevertheless provide a moderate safeguard against less dangerous threats such as SARS-CoV, SARS-CoV-2, MERS, flu, etc.

Such an approach does not require that the vulnerable population is identified months or weeks in advance, as is the case if pathogen-specific vaccines are employed as prophylactic measures. A rapid-acting approach increases the likelihood of preventing disease symptoms from developing because it expands the window in which prophylaxis will be successful. Apart from being nonspecific, such a broad-spectrum approach can be applied universally even without a potential threat, which in the case of an unexpected threat will work independently of the incubation period length. A successful approach must be sufficiently long-lasting so that the frequency of its administration does not present an overwhelming organizational burden to medical professionals. As well, if the approach chosen is developed in such a way that it has long-lasting character, this will significantly reduce long-term population protection costs.

Approaches that are effective against a broad spectrum of infectious agents will eliminate the limitations of specificity that existing chemoprophylaxis and vaccines have. Such approaches can be used as pre-exposure and post-exposure prophylaxes even when the infectious agent has not yet been conclusively identified. Furthermore, an approach that is relatively easy to deliver is essential to address the logistics of a limited number of medical personnel administering prophylaxis to an enormous target population.

This approach should not cause concern among the population because some of its additional advantages are

- enhanced individual and herd immunity against common infections such as influenza, streptococcal and staphylococcal infections, Coxsackievirus infection, Lyme disease, and many others;

- some degree of protection against some immunity-dependent noncommunicable diseases such as cancer, autoimmune diseases, neurodegenerative diseases, etc.;

- an increased proportion of able-bodied population as a result of the first two advantages;

- a reduced rate of maternal and child mortality because a high proportion of such deaths are caused by either infectious diseases or abnormal maternal immune activation resulting from infection; and

- possible increased populational life expectancy due to the abovementioned benefits and mortality reduction.

Some available means of protection are already long-lasting, broad spectrum, and rapid-acting, and these will be discussed later in the chapter. However, these means were not intentionally developed for broad-spectrum protection; rather, this peculiarity was discovered years after their application as specific protection measures, so they are only moderately effective in infectious disease prevention. However, using the same mechanism underlying these beneficial characteristics of the available products, more powerful tools can be successfully developed.

INNATE VS. ADAPTIVE IMMUNITY

Before discussing broad-spectrum prophylactic measures, immunity in general should be explained.

Immunity is differentiated into two types: innate and adaptive.

Innate immunity is considered an effective and robust defense against infection, and the reaction of the innate immune system to a pathogen often predetermines the outcome of a disease. Innate immunity is nonspecific, meaning the same types of cells and molecules are immediately produced in response to all viral and bacterial infections. The innate immunity response is mediated by a number of cells and compounds. Dendritic cells and macrophages are the first cellular components of the innate immune system responsible for the antiviral response. Some other components of the innate immune system include white blood cells, natural killer cells, interferons, and other cytokines. Innate immunity is a type of immune response induced upon the first sign of an infection. For some infections, a rapid innate immunity response can be strong enough to eliminate the infection without allowing it to develop into the disease. On the other hand, the innate immune response can suppress the infection effectively enough until the adaptive immune response is activated and developed. Young and healthy people have a more rapidly reacting and functional innate immunity that demonstrates a timely response to a viral pathogen. Thus, it either does not allow the infection to occur or suppresses the viral replication. So, thanks to the normal functioning of innate immunity, young and healthy people generally do not have severe symptoms and survive the infection.

Adaptive immunity is a type of immunity that is more effective in infection suppression due to high-specificity protective proteins that can protect only against a specific virus or bacterium. But cells belonging to the adaptive immune system, such as T-cells and antibody-producing B-cells, take more time to be produced. So, a rapid and sufficiently strong innate immune response and a timely adaptive immune response are two elements of effective natural protection.

INTERFERONS FOR ANTIVIRAL DEFENSE

The most interesting molecules among immune system agents are interferons (IFNs). These signaling proteins interfere with viral invasion via several mechanisms, activating other components of the immune system, modulating the antiviral activity of other cells, and fighting viral particles directly at every step of infection.

IFNs are naturally produced by immune cells. Their production can be enhanced by so-called IFN inducers. Apart from this, there are exogenous interferons that are administered to prevent or support the immune response to infections.

Type I IFNs regulate a number of essential processes during host antiviral defense. Individuals with impaired or reduced type I IFN production and signaling are susceptible to viral infections. IFN-α and IFN-γ work by binding their receptors and activating downstream antiviral pathways involving the dsRNA-dependent protein kinase (PKR), the 2′,5′ oligoadenylate synthetase/ RNase L, or the MxA protein. dsRNA, ssRNA, and CpG oligonucleotides are ligands for toll-like receptors (TLRs) and modulate antiviral immunity through TLR signaling pathways and IFN induction. It is also known that, apart from directly interfering with viral replication, IFNs also affect antigen-presenting cells to stimulate antigen presentation to T-cells through the MHC upregulation. As well, IFN-gamma has a number of overlapping functions with type I IFNs, but in addition it interferes with every stage of virus life, from entry and replication to release, transmission, and reactivation.

The effectiveness of IFNs was well shown for infection prevention (but not treatment). It is well known that the severity of infection depends on the IFNs' response timing relative to infection. Immediate production of one's own type I IFNs or exogenous IFN administration can result in clearance of the virus or in a delayed and slowed multiplication, easing the symptoms. On the other hand, a delay in type I IFN response will most likely result in the increase of pro-inflammatory cytokine production and more severe outcomes. Numerous studies have proved experimentally that IFNs inhibit many infections, including SARS-CoV (reduction of plaque formation by up to 30-fold and reduced replication rate by up to 3,000-fold). Prophylactic intranasal administration of IFNs can effectively prevent the coronaviral infection in about 70% of people, and the remaining infected individuals usually tend to have several times less severe symptoms and a shorter infection duration.

Bearing in mind that many infections' peculiarity is a prolonged incubation period, which makes it more difficult to take corresponding measures, preventive instruments should provide enhanced production of IFNs. Thus, it is logical to use interferon inducers as the most appropriate preventive measure.

AVAILABLE SOLUTIONS

The solutions discussed in this section are also vaccines, but contrary to most vaccines, the limitations of which were discussed above, the live vaccines discussed below in addition to effective pathogen-specific protection also provide long-lasting nonspecific defense via stimulation of the immune system's ability to respond rapidly and effectively to different infectious agents.

One such solution is the Bacillus Calmette-Guérin (BCG) vaccine, a live attenuated tuberculosis vaccine. A recent finding that is being actively discussed today shows that countries without universal policies of BCG vaccination (e.g., Italy, the Netherlands, the United States) have been more severely affected by COVID-19 compared to countries with universal and long-standing BCG policies. At the same time, countries that have been late in beginning a universal BCG policy show higher mortality among COVID-19 patients, consistent with the idea that BCG protects the vaccinated population.

In the late 1920s, the nonspecific effect of the BCG vaccine became obvious soon after its discovery. Due to the vaccine's nonspecific immune effects, it halves the overall all-cause mortality among newborns because it prevents about 30% of infections by any pathogen, not only tuberculosis. As well, BCG revaccination with a preceding diphtheria, tetanus toxoids, and pertussis (DTP) vaccination can additionally halve mortality in older children. The mechanism of the BCG vaccine's nonspecific action is enhancement of innate immunity. The most important nonspecific effect of this vaccine, responsible for protection from infection, is the induction of enhanced production of IFNs and natural killer (NK) cells.

It is worth noting once again that in the Unites States, the BCG is not commonly administered due to the low risk of infection with *Mycobacterium tuberculosis* and its interference with tuberculin skin test reactivity.

Based on the same principle of cross-reactivity, it is worth considering another, potentially even more effective, solution: smallpox vaccination using new-generation vaccines (e.g., the Modified Vaccinia Ankara, or MVA) that are safe and have gained approval in the United States and Canada. The smallpox vaccine is also known to have a so-called para-immune effect, i.e., it is capable of providing nonspecific immune protection against many other infections. For instance, relatively recently, it became known that the risk of HIV infection among smallpox-vaccinated individuals is about two times lower than among unvaccinated ones. Similarly, as with the BCG, the all-cause mortality rate among vaccinated adults is on average 40% lower. The first and foremost mechanism of nonspecific protection provided by smallpox vaccines is the induction of nonspecific innate immunity via increased production of IFNs that can last for *up to 60 years.*

Both the BCG and MVA vaccines have been proven safe by dozens of studies. Some time ago, most citizens of the United States received smallpox vaccines, but vaccination stopped in 1972 after the eradication of smallpox. The BCG vaccine was never universal in the United States, but in many other countries it was among the vaccines recommended for everyone.

As discussed in one of the previous sections, these vaccines were not intentionally developed to provide nonspecific immunity against a broad spectrum of infections, but it appeared to be a fortuitous additional benefit. However, these means are already available and tested, and some countries, like Australia, have already started using this knowledge in the context of the COVID-19 pandemic to protect medical workers, who are among the most vulnerable individuals. On the other hand, this knowledge can be used to create more sophisticated broad-spectrum vaccines, but with the specific intention of ensuring effective population protection against unexpected threats.

ADDITIONAL CONSIDERATIONS

In addition to the potential defense tools discussed above, it is important to mention another factor affecting population susceptibility to infectious agents. In the case of most infections, the most vulnerable populations are elderly people and those with preexisting chronic conditions such as cancer, cardiovascular disease, chronic respiratory and autoimmune diseases, etc. It is a well-known fact that aging and the abovementioned diseases and conditions are accompanied by chronic inflammation and insufficiency and dysregulation of the immune system response. This results in the immune system's inability to suppress and fight infections. It is known that elevated levels of proinflammatory mediators (C-reactive protein, tumor necrosis factor, interleukins 1-beta and 6) are associated with infectious disease-caused mortality in these people. Apart from this, the elevation of proinflammatory mediators also negatively affects hemoglobin concentrations; insulin-like growth factor 1 levels; and levels of albumin, micronutrients, and vitamins.

Some changes in the immune system observed in people with chronic low-grade inflammation include

- reduced phagocytic activity and number of monocytes and macrophages,
- reduction in MHC II expression,
- altered cytokines production,
- altered TLR expression and signaling,
- decreased natural killer (NK) cells cytotoxic activity,
- dysfunctional neutrophils,
- decreased number of naïve T and B cells,
- increased accumulation of senescent T cells, and
- diminished response of T cells to new antigens.

The combination of these immune abnormalities is known as immuno-aging. This condition is characterized by dysregulation of both the innate and adaptive immune systems. Malfunctioning of the immune system in the respiratory system of these individuals is especially well described, which is especially important since the most effective types of bioweapons are those disseminated by aerosols. In regard to pulmonary immunity, elevated levels of proinflammatory mediators contribute to diminished pulmonary function and dysregulate immune responses to respiratory infections, which are characterized by reduced mucociliary clearance, upregulation of proteins participating in the attachment of pathogens to epithelial cells of the respiratory system, reduction of TLR expression on lung cells, etc. In addition to the numerous immune system alterations increasing susceptibility to respiratory infections, existing lung inflammatory responses upon new infection also increase susceptibility to bacterial coinfections such as *Streptococcus pneumoniae* and others.

As a matter of fact, the initial immune response plays a crucial role in the infectious disease outcome. For instance, in viral infections, cells generally respond to infection by mounting an innate antiviral response to limit the spread of the infection and aid in inducing an adaptive immune response that will eventually clear the virus. Coronaviruses exploit the toll-like and some other receptors for initial attachment. Activation of one or more of these sensors generally leads to the activation of the transcription factors IFN-regulatory factors 3 and 7 and NF-κB. These stimulate the expression and excretion of type-I IFN and pro-inflammatory cytokines, which in turn activate the JAK-STAT signaling cascade that induces the expression of antiviral interferon-stimulated genes (ISGs). This ultimately results in an antiviral state in the infected and neighboring cells. ISGs were shown to target virtually all steps of the viral cycle in order to restrict viral replication. However, it was found that TLRs are downregulated in the condition of immuno-aging. Dysregulated immune responses drive the respiratory infections' hallmark syndromes, such as acute respiratory distress syndrome (ARDS), cytokine release syndrome (CRS), and lymphopenia.

Thus, the overall patterns of infection spread and mortality in countries depends on the chronic diseases' prevalence. Our research of COVID-19 incidence and mortality dependence on the prevalence of chronic diseases shows that there is a positive correlation between both incidence and mortality among countries. This does not indicate that only people affected by cancer, cardiovascular disease, or other associated comorbidities have increased COVID-19 mortality, but also those with chronic low-grade inflammation resulting from immuno-aging, which just has not resulted in a specific disease yet.

Most developed countries have a very high rate of chronic inflammation and up to 96% of the population die due to conditions caused by chronic inflammation. In the United States, this figure is 88%. According to the WHO, "Currently, chronic diseases are by far the leading cause of death in the world and their impact is steadily growing. The report projects that approximately 17 million people die prematurely each year as a result of the global epidemic of chronic disease."[114]

Although the chronic diseases we discuss here are also called chronic noncommunicable diseases, there is still accumulated knowledge regarding the role of chronic persistent and latent bacterial and viral infections in these diseases. It is not widespread knowledge, but a large proportion of the population are carriers of chronic bacterial and viral infections, which are usually the main cause of chronic inflammation in addition to other, secondary factors such as diet and nutrition, lifestyle, pollution, etc. For instance, in some developed countries, the overall asymptomatic chronic carriage of *N. meningitidis*, a respiratory pathogen, reaches 60%. Ignoring this problem means placing people with these problems (the largest proportion of the population) at risk of dying of an unexpected infectious threat because these people's immune system is unable to respond to an infection effectively.

The situation with COVID-19 in the United States has revealed an outcome that can be expected as a result of any other infectious threat— high incidence and mortality rates because people affected and deceased during this pandemic are people who are generally vulnerable to infection. This indicates a critical need for solutions to reduce chronic inflammation and fight chronic infections because any other means of prevention will lose its effectiveness due to widespread abnormal immune response.

ALTERNATIVE METHODS OF POPULATION PROTECTION

Among currently available diagnostic, preventive, and treatment measures, several are worth mentioning. Numerous studies, case reports, and clinical trials have already shown that the treatment of infections may have a highly beneficial health effect in relation to chronic diseases.

Clinics in many countries do not evaluate main inflammatory markers as part of routine tests. The widespread testing of known markers and the creation of new diagnostic approaches and methods to assess systemic inflammation or its individual branches will help prevent the emergence of chronic disease or allow it to be treated in the early stages, thus protecting the population not only from chronic noncommunicable diseases but also from potential infectious threats.

Although there is no universally established criterion, the tests below can help in detecting the pro-inflammatory state.

- Blood and/or saliva
  o C-reactive protein
  o IL-6
  o Ferritin level
  o TNF-alpha
  o Fibrinogen level
- Blood
  o Hemoglobin A1C
  o Erythrocyte count and sedimentation rate
  o Lymphocyte count
  o Neutrophil count
  o White blood cell count
  o Creatine kinase

Despite the already relatively well-established understanding of chronic inflammation, medical science and practice for the treatment of chronic inflammation still do not exist. The list of drugs used to treat these pathologies is very short, and the creation of integrated approaches to anti-inflammatory therapy, combined with effective anti-infectious treatment, can significantly prevent premature deaths promoted by the abovementioned conditions.

Antibacterial and antiviral therapies were shown to help people with such "non-infectious" diseases as lymphoma, leukemia, breast cancer, glioblastoma, hepatocellular carcinomas, nasopharyngeal cancer, diabetes type 2, atherosclerosis, and other pathologies. To explain this effect and its relevance to biodefense issues more clearly:

1. These chronic diseases are a result of chronic inflammation.
2. Chronic inflammation is often a result of chronic infectious disease.
3. At the same time, chronic inflammation is a factor leading to immune system dysregulation.
4. Immune system dysregulation is a factor making people more vulnerable to infectious threats, both naturally occurring and deliberate.
5. Antiviral/antibacterial treatment helps people with these chronic diseases.
6. This indicates that the infectious agents causing these diseases were eradicated or suppressed, which led to reduction of chronic inflammation.
7. Thus, treatment of people with antibiotics/antivirals will help them reduce their inflammation and modulate their immune system functioning. As a result, these people will be less susceptible to potential infectious threats from both biological weapons and natural epidemics.

CONCLUSION

The COVID-19 pandemic has revealed an underestimation of the damage that can be caused by an infectious threat. This indicates an urgent need for the development of novel approaches in biodefense. Existing pathogen-specific pre- and post-exposure protection means did not prove to be a feasible option, and thus an alternative approach that targets immune stimulation may be an option to diminish the negative effect of another unexpected epidemic or attack. This approach should be rapid-acting, broad-spectrum, and long-lasting, and vaccines with a para-immune effect can be such an option.

At the same time, chronic inflammation, which plays a role in increased mortality from any infection, is a serious problem and is very likely to be detrimental to survival during any other unexpected epidemic or attack. In order to reduce losses due to unexpected infectious threats, there is a necessity to reconsider more comprehensive methods of chronic inflammation diagnosis, prevention, and treatment of these conditions to protect the population.

9.

INTERNATIONAL BIOLOGICAL DEFENSE AND VERIFICATION

By Paula A. DeSutter

T he COVID-19 pandemic and the uncertainty surrounding its onset have raised a number of questions: Can international biological defense efforts aid the challenge of verifying whether a nation— in this case, China—has violated its international arms control obligations banning the production of offensive biological and toxin weapons and their use? What are those obligations? What is verification of noncompliance and how is it done in the United States? What organizations are involved in the international biodefense effort? How reliable is the evidence these organizations collect? Can COVID-19 be investigated as a possible use of biological weapons to exercise U.S. and global capabilities to investigate and analyze future use in violation of

Paula DeSutter gives a press conference at the State Department in 2008.

existing arms control obligations? Here, we will explore the answers to these questions and their implications.

INTERNATIONAL PROHIBITIONS ON OFFENSIVE BIOLOGICAL AND TOXIN WEAPONS PROGRAMS AND USE OF SUCH WEAPONS IN WAR

Two international agreements prohibit the use of biological agents (in warfare): the 1925 Geneva Protocol and the 1972 Biological and Toxin Weapons Convention.

The 1925 Geneva Protocol. The 1925 Geneva Protocol for the Prohibition of the Use in War of Asphyxiating, Poisonous or Other Gases, and of Bacteriological Methods of Warfare, was ratified by U.S. President Gerald Ford on January 22, 1975. Its key provisions state:

> Whereas the use in war of asphyxiating, poisonous or other gases, and of all analogous liquids, materials or devices, has been justly condemned by the general opinion of the civilized world;

> the High Contracting Parties, so far as they are not already Parties to Treaties prohibiting such use, accept this prohibition, agree to extend this prohibition to the use of bacteriological methods of warfare and agree to be bound as between themselves according to the terms of this declaration.

> ...The present Protocol will come into force for each signatory Power as from the date of deposit of its ratification, and, from that moment, each Power will be bound as regards other Powers which have already deposited their ratifications.

The People's Republic of China acceded to the Protocol by means of a declaration of succession on July 13, 1952.

The 1972 Biological and Toxin Weapons Convention. The 1972 Convention on the Prohibition of the Development, Production and Stockpiling of Bacteriological (Biological) and Toxin Weapons and On Their Destruction, also known as the BWC, took effect in 1975.

Its key parts state:

Article I

Each State Party to this Convention undertakes never in any circumstances to develop, produce, stockpile or otherwise acquire or retain:

(1) microbial or other biological agents, or toxins whatever their origin or method of production, of types and in quantities that have no justification for prophylactic, protective or other peaceful purposes

(2) weapons, equipment or means of delivery designed to use such agents or toxins for hostile purposes or in armed conflict

Article II

Each State Party to this Convention undertakes to destroy, or to divert to peaceful purposes, as soon as possible but not later than nine months after the entry into force of the Convention, all agents, toxins, weapons, equipment and means of delivery specified in Article I of the Convention, which are in its possession or under its jurisdiction or control. In implementing the provisions of this Article all necessary safety precautions shall be observed to protect populations and the environment.

Article III

Each State Party to this Convention undertakes not to transfer to any recipient whatsoever, directly or indirectly, and not in any way to assist, encourage, or induce any State, group of States or international organizations to manufacture or otherwise acquire any of the agents, toxins, weapons, equipment or means of delivery specified in Article I of the Convention,

Article IV

Each State Party to this Convention shall, in accordance with its constitutional processes, take any necessary measures to prohibit and prevent the development, production, stockpiling, acquisition or retention the agents, toxins, weapons, equipment and means of delivery specified in Article I of the Convention, within the territory of such State, under its jurisdiction or under its control anywhere.

China acceded to the Convention on November 15, 1984, and since that time has been legally obligated to abide by its terms.

TABLE 1

Topics Covered by State Parties' Submissions on Relevant Developments in Science and Technology to the Biological and Toxin Weapons Convention 2011 Review Conference

Topic	State(s)
Advances in manipulation of genetic material and microorganisms and in understanding of pathogenicity	United States of America
Antiviral peptides discovery	Poland
Awareness-raising communication, confidence-building, and scientific conduct	United States of America
Bioinformatics	Germany, United Kingdom, United States
Biological production technologies	United Kingdom
Bioreactors	South Africa
Biosensors	Czech Republic, South Africa
Convergence of biology and chemistry	Australia
Creation of manmade pathogens	**China**
De novo synthesis of organisms	South Africa
Decontamination	United Kingdom
Diagnostics and epidemiology	South Africa
Disease detection, identification, and monitoring technology	Czech Republic
Disease surveillance, sensor, and detection technologies	United Kingdom, United States
Dispersal technology	South Africa, United Kingdom

Topic	State(s)
Drug delivery systems	Germany, United Kingdom, United States
Export control and border security technologies	United States of America
Genetic engineering of viruses	Poland
Genomics laying the foundations for pathogen transformation	**China**
Genomics, proteomics, and other "-omics"	United Kingdom
High-throughput whole-genome sequencing	Sweden
Improvements in biosafety and biosecurity practices	United States of America
Industrial application of biotechnology – disposable equipment	United States of America
Medical countermeasures	United Kingdom, United States of America
Microbial forensics	China, Czech Republic, Sweden, United Kingdom, United States of America
Nanotechnology	Czech Republic, Netherlands, South Africa, United Kingdom, United States
Neuroscience	South Africa, United Kingdom
Novel therapeutics	Czech Republic
Population-specific genetic markers	**China**
Simulants and software	Portugal
Specific experiments of concern	South Africa
Strengthening of laboratory capacity	Portugal
Synthetic biology	China, Germany, Netherlands, South Africa, United Kingdom
Systems biology	China, South Africa, United Kingdom[115]
Targeted drug-delivery technology making it easier to spread pathogens	**China**
Vaccine development	Poland, South Africa
Visualization technology	Czech Republic

CHALLENGES TO VERIFICATION OF THE BWC

Table 1 is a list of some of the challenges of assessing compliance with the BWC, which are further explained below.

Concealment. First, unless a nation wishes to bring international attention to its noncompliance with *any* agreement, it will seek to conceal its noncompliant activities. Constrained or prohibited activities, such as the launch of a long-range ballistic missile, may be difficult to conceal, while others are easier to conceal. Items or activities that can take place in facilities that may hide their purpose from overhead satellite imagery cannot be detected and verified unless the verifying party receives some sort of "tip-off" from other sources of information that indicates something illicit is taking place at that location. Even then, intelligence sources and methods may not be able to provide evidence that prohibited activity is taking place.

Prohibiting or impeding access. Even if an agreement calls for on-site inspections, the inspected parties, as sovereign nations, can impede or preclude even the oft-advocated "anytime, anywhere" or "challenge" type of inspections from finding the truth. Such inspections are not conducted by black helicopters flying wherever they want over a sovereign power's territory, interviewing participants or witnesses without interference, and confiscating evidence. The host nation always provides the transportation and controls access to locations and people. The host nation decides who is allowed on the inspection teams, what equipment they may bring, and what, if anything, may be taken out of the country for testing.

The 1925 Geneva Protocol and customary international law govern the use of chemical or toxin agents "in war." Investigations of agent use in the midst of a war is dangerous at best, and investigators would presumably need to be granted access by one or more of the belligerent parties. Depending on whether the evidence of use can be weakened by time or covered up, lack of timeliness may work against the credibility of inspection results.

Unless a state party to the BWC seeks an international investigation to demonstrate its compliance, which one would expect a fully compliant state party to do, no inspections are provided for in the BWC. While for a time some nations advocated adding inspection requirements to the

BWC, for the reasons addressed below, it is not clear that such treaty-mandated inspections could provide internationally agreed evidence of noncompliance.

Dual-use activities present special challenges to verification. The dual-use nature of biological activities provides a ready avenue for hiding or denying an offensive biological weapons program. If a nation is violating the BWC, presumably it would only do so if it viewed the violations as worth the consequences of any possible verification of the violation. Given that the violation would almost certainly be a high-value national priority, the violating party would certainly go to the trouble of constructing a web of denial in the form of justification of the activity as being for purely prophylactic, protective, and peaceful purposes.

Because the BWC permits the development and production of biological agents "of types and in quantities" that have justification for prophylactic, protective, or other peaceful purposes, it is also necessary to have sufficient evidence that the purpose of activities of concern can be established as not credibly for peaceful purposes alone.

It is necessary, in assessing compliance with the BWC, to construct a "circumstantial evidence" case in which many pieces of evidence, when woven together, produce one pattern above the others. For those in the United States and elsewhere who hold to a "beyond a shadow of doubt" standard of evidence, no violation of the BWC could ever be established. If no violation can ever be established, any prohibitions or restrictions in the agreement are rendered meaningless.

Despite this challenge, the United States has detected violations of the BWC after constructing circumstantial evidence cases and using a standard of evidence more akin to a "preponderance of evidence." In one case, the United States was able to establish that a country had pursued a technology particularly well suited for dissemination of a biological agent it was known to be producing. In another case, multiple pieces of evidence, including evidence of open-air testing of an agent against staked animals, was used in the assessment. In one particular case, the United States assessed that the Soviet Union had transferred and assisted a non-party in the use of toxin weapons.

Traditionally, we have believed that the most obvious evidence of an offensive biological or toxin weapons program would be the use of a biological agent. Even in such a case, however, the United States can expect controversy since some believe that even a bizarre alternative explanation casts doubt on the U.S. government's assessments based on all-source intelligence and other evidence. Such was the case when the United States assessed that the Soviet Union provided mycotoxins and assistance to its clients in Laos and Kampuchea, and chemical agents for use in Afghanistan. While controversial at the time and dismissed now by those who never reviewed all the evidence available to the U.S. government, the use as alleged was found by the United States to be inconsistent with the 1925 Geneva Protocol as it reflects customary international law.

WHAT IS VERIFICATION OF NONCOMPLIANCE AND HOW IS IT DONE IN THE UNITED STATES?

Verification is a policy process in which relevant information, or evidence, of the actions of parties related to international obligations are weighed against those legal obligations to assess whether or not the party is violating its obligations. The United States uses all available information from all sources to make this determination, but particularly from intelligence sources and methods. Generally, a single source of information is inadequate to reach a finding that another party to an agreement has violated it. The evidence must be weighed against the obligations.

The effectiveness of verification depends greatly on the clarity of the language of the legal obligations and political commitments, on our ability to collect intelligence and other information relevant to an assessment of the obligations, and on the standards of evidence used in assessing noncompliance. Regarding the standard of evidence, the unclassified summary report of the General Advisory Committee (the GAC) to the President on Arms Control and Disarmament, which was submitted to Congress in October 1984, states that

> past analyses (other than the President's report to the Congress of January 23, 1984) have tended to invoke standards of proof applicable only when powers to collect and to inspect evidence, to subpoena witnesses, to take testimony under oath, to prosecute for perjury, etc., are available as legal tools.[116]

For the United States, verification and compliance assessments have been mandated by law since the Fiscal Year 1984 Arms Control and Disarmament Act, although the law mandated only assessments of Soviet noncompliance[117] until the 1990s.

The first finding in the first congressionally mandated presidential report on noncompliance concerned Soviet violation of its obligations under the BWC and the 1925 Geneva Protocol and related rules of customary international law. The GAC Report reached the same conclusion.

CHINESE NONCOMPLIANCE WITH THE BWC

In 1987, Senator Claiborne Pell of the Senate Foreign Relations Committee sought to change the focus of the annual reports to Congress on Soviet noncompliance with arms control treaties. He amended the Arms Control and Disarmament Act to require the executive branch to address questions that had arisen regarding U.S. compliance and to identify actions taken by the Soviet Union to comply with obligations, in addition to questions about the noncompliance of the Soviet Union "and other countries."[118]

In the June 1992 Pell Report, which addressed concerns regarding the use of chemical weapons by Iraq and regarding other cases of possible use of chemical weapons, the report stated that "recent actions in the Persian Gulf led the United States to examine new issues in this section of the October 1991 Report. These issues concern compliance with the 1972 Biological and Toxin Weapons Convention."[119] No information was provided in either the 1991 or 1992 reports. The first report to address specific countries was the January 1993 report, which combined the Adherence to and Compliance with Arms Control and the President's Report to the Congress on Soviet Noncompliance. That report stated that

> the United States government believes that based on available evidence, China maintained an offensive BW program throughout most of the 1980s. The offensive BW program included the development, production, stockpiling or other acquisition or maintenance of biological warfare agents. China's CBM mandated declarations have not resolved US concerns about this program and there are

strong indications that China probably maintains its offensive program. The United States Government, therefore, believes that in the years after its accession to the BWC, China was not in compliance with its BWC obligations and that it is highly probable that it remains noncompliant with these obligations.[120]

The essence of this finding has been maintained in the years since 1993. The 2005 Noncompliance Report explained that

The United States believes that China began its offensive BW program in the 1950s and continued its program throughout the Cold War, even after China acceded to the BWC in 1984. Undoubtedly China perceived a threat from the BW programs of its neighbor, the Soviet Union. There are some reports that China may still retain elements of its biological warfare program. Such reports support the United States' continued belief that China has not abandoned its offensive BW program.[121]

Facilities of particular concern were identified. The report also noted that

from 1993 to the present, military scientists have published in open literature the results of studies of aerosol stability of bacteria, models of infectious virus aerosols, and detection of aerosolized viruses using polymerase chain reaction technology. Such advanced biotechnology techniques could be applicable to the development of offensive BW agents and weapons.

The "CBM mandated declarations" referred to in the 1993 finding were initially agreed on at the Second Review Conference for the BWC in 1986. It was agreed that the parties would exchange confidence-building measures (CBMs) "in order to prevent or reduce the occurrence of ambiguities, doubts and suspicions and in order to improve international cooperation in the field of peaceful biological activities." The CBMs were expanded during a meeting of scientific and technical experts in 1987 and were modified and considerably expanded by the Third Review Conference in 1991.

Since in Article II of the BWC each State Party to the Convention agrees to "destroy, or to divert to peaceful purposes, as soon as possible but not later than nine months after the entry into force of the Convention, all agents, toxins, weapons, equipment and means of delivery," the CBMs since 1991 have called on the State Parties to declare, among other things, their past offensive activities.

While China submits its annual CBM data declarations every year, including in 2020, the United States knows the information China provides is inaccurate and misleading since China has never admitted that it ever had an offensive biological weapons program, and much less that it has taken any steps to eliminate the program. On the contrary, China insists it never had such a program at all.

Pablo Picasso said that "art is the lie that reveals the truth." So it is that the Chinese false CBM declarations are the lie that reveals the truth of their violation of the BWC, and their lack of transparency and truthfulness.

The Chinese, however, have sought to use the BWC and the processes for collaboration and review to represent China as a fully compliant state party. Still, the BWC processes have resulted in some observations that may reveal more about their biological weapons activities than they intended.

China's submission under the heading "New scientific and technological developments relevant to the Convention" at the 2011 BWC Review Conference is couched in terms that seemingly highlight legitimate concerns regarding the risks of some of the major advancements in biotechnology. However, the Chinese submission differed significantly from the submissions of other Parties. For example, the following table, reproduced in its entirety, was compiled by Dr. Piers D. Millett in a chapter for an online publication funded by the Canadian government.[122] A comparison of the topics addressed by countries other than China, or by China when working with other nations, with those addressed by China alone, highlighted in bold, is greatly concerning. The topics addressed by China alone include "Creation of manmade pathogens," "Genomics laying the foundations for pathogen transformation," "Population-specific genetic markers," and "Targeted drug-delivery technology making it easier to spread pathogens."

COVID-19 INVESTIGATION

At least in theory, and particularly in light of China's noncompliance with the BWC, investigation of the outbreak might provide the world with a template for international investigations and collection and reporting of evidence of possible use of biological, toxin, or chemical agents. The questions that must be evaluated include, with what certainty and in how timely a manner can the organization conduct an investigation, particularly if the host country has some complicity in use, and how reliable is the information reported by current organizations?

International investigations of infectious outbreaks have been done in the past, such as that of the severe acute respiratory syndrome (SARS), Middle East respiratory syndrome (MERS), H1N1 influenza, or Ebola outbreaks in primarily the Democratic Republic of the Congo in Africa.

Most investigatory bodies, including the WHO and the U.S. CDC, the Bipartisan Commission on Biodefense, can only conduct investigations if they are invited by the host nations where outbreaks are occurring. These investigations are primarily focused on identifying the nature of the disease and its transmission, recommending actions to limit transmission of the disease, and identifying treatment options. The same is true of Doctors without Borders. Other international organizations, like INTERPOL, are primarily concerned with interdicting or investigating possible future or current bioterrorism activities.

On May 19, 2020, the WHO member states agreed to a resolution introduced by the European Union to require an independent probe into the UN agency's coronavirus response. The United States and other nations' criticism mounted in recent weeks over the WHO's handling of the pandemic. As discussed in previous chapters and articulated in the president's May 18, 2020, letter to the director-general of the WHO, China's denials and cover-up of evidence, with the seeming cooperation of the director-general, has resulted in a pandemic that has led to hundreds of thousands of deaths globally as well as a severe economic downturn.

However, the development of international investigatory efforts *may* offer new sources of evidence of use of biological or toxin weapons, since in the case of an infectious disease a single infected person may be used as a vector or weapon.

CONCLUSION

Can international biological defense efforts aid the challenge of verifying whether a nation has violated its international arms control obligations banning the production of offensive biological and toxin weapons and their use? They may be new sources of information, but it remains to be seen whether their investigations will, without being so directed, pursue elements of investigation regarding possible violation of the BWC or 1925 Geneva Protocol.

This is because questions that aren't asked are seldom answered.

It is not probable that COVID-19 represents a case of China unleashing a biological weapon on the world. It is, however, possible. Unfortunately, nations have been known to perpetrate evil actions against their own populations and against other nations. The COVID-19 pandemic is devastating enough to life and treasure that it should be investigated as a possible case, if for no other reason than to exercise the U.S. and global system's capability to conduct a credible-use investigation.

10.

THE U.S. BIODEFENSE STRATEGY IN THE TIME OF COVID: REALITY INTRUDES ON POLICY

By Stephen A. Elliott

America's first comprehensive strategy to defend the nation against biological threats became policy on September 18, 2018, when the Trump administration released the National Biodefense Strategy. Mandated by Congress in the 2017 National Defense Authorization Act, the strategy

coordinates all federal government biodefense efforts. It creates a vision and a purpose and defines how the United States should anticipate and respond to biodefense threats.

For those expecting a detailed discussion of biodefense threats and potential solutions, however, this strategy is a great disappointment. Rather than being a real strategy, the document is instead a detailed litany of things the government should do, things that it should analyze, and goals toward which it should aspire.

Reception

Even before the publication of the Strategy, which we will call the NBS, there was opposition to its release. One commentator believed a national strategy would only add to the confusion and not lead to action, while increasing budgets. Moreover, some argued various threats, such as public health, economic disruption, and biological attack, require different policies for each threat.[123]

Despite this, the NBS was generally greeted with support and a recognition that it addressed all aspects of biodefense, particularly public health and defense against biological attack. Some commentators noted that funding was not a part of the policy, and as one critic put it, "the administration's actions do not match its words."[124]

The Bipartisan Commission on Biodefense, chaired by the first Homeland Security Secretary, Governor Tom Ridge, praised the release of NBS but said it was "a great start."[125] This praise was tempered with a recognition that a great deal of follow-up and funding were necessary. These concerns appeared to be confirmed with the outbreak of COVID-19, which highlighted the NBS's limitations.

Strategy Overview

The most notable principle in the document is the broad scope that includes all biological incidents: natural disease outbreaks, laboratory accidents, and deliberate biological attacks. It states that whether an outbreak is naturally occurring or not, the response will be the same.

While COVID-19 appears to be a naturally occurring virus, it is unclear at this writing whether it originated from an accident in a laboratory or is a naturally occurring viral outbreak. Nonetheless, our intense response to the COVID-19 pandemic was implemented despite not knowing its origin. The NBS recognizes the importance of not segregating the cause of outbreak from the response.

Another key principle is that biological threats are not only about healthcare, but pose economic and social threats. Until 2020 this was seen as only a theoretical risk. COVID-19 has proved with startling clarity that there are real economic and social impacts to biological and disease vents.

The NBS also recognizes that a bio-incident is a national security issue.[126] As a result, while the Secretary of Health and Human Services is identified as the chair of the Biodefense Steering Committee (which includes eight cabinet members), the National Security Advisor is identified as the lead on biodefense policy coordination. While it is somewhat unclear where the line is drawn between the National Security Council and the Steering Committee, the recognition that a public health issue is also a national security issue is clear in the document.

It should be noted that when such a bio-incident occurred as a result of the COVID-19 pandemic, neither the National Security Advisor nor the Secretary of Health and Human Services was in charge. Instead, the president was involved personally, with the vice president as chair of the Coronavirus Taskforce.

The Strategy lays out five goals of our biodefense program: (1) risk awareness, (2) increased response capability, (3) mitigation planning, (4) information sharing, and (5) economic and social recovery.

Goals and Objectives

Goal 1: Enable risk awareness to inform decision-making across the biodefense enterprise. The focus of this goal ensures that we encourage research and the sharing of information about potential biological events. In particular, the NBS discusses forecasting. The wild swings in forecasting during the COVID-19 pandemic show the importance of this objective. Traditionally, we have relied upon the CDC, the Bipartisan Commission on Biodefense or other government agencies for forecasting, but it is clear the federal government lacks the capability to perform accurate forecasting. The result was that academia, state governments and some federal agencies all produced forecasting models so disparate that planning became difficult. The media reported all of these disparate forecasts as hard facts even as those "facts" shifted, undermined public confidence, and misplaced resources. Take, for example, the forecast of the number of ventilators needed. Governor Andrew Cuomo of New York stated that 40,000 were needed in his state, and some said the United States overall would need hundreds of thousands of them. New York eventually only needed about 5,000; the entire country needed only about 16,000 at the height of the pandemic.

That number is about equal to what we had at the beginning of the outbreak.

The Trump administration, however, relied upon various forecasts to order enough ventilators based on the most pessimistic forecasts. By the end of 2020, the Unites States will have 200,000 ventilators at a cost of $3 billion.[127] While having a large stockpile of ventilators is not a bad idea, having more than 10 times what we needed during the height of a major pandemic and spending $3 billion to do so is not the kind of "informed decision-making" that the strategy anticipated.

While even these forecasts can be valuable tools in planning, using forecasts for specific government contract planning is not the proper usage of such information. However, for planning information related to a biological incident, such forecasts can be valuable if used for the right purposes.[128]

A recent analysis in the *New England Journal of Medicine* noted that such forecasts are necessarily based on ranges and trends rather than hard planning. According to the study from the Center for Communicable Disease Dynamics at Harvard,

> uncertainty in a key epidemiologic parameter or set of parameters—the duration of infectiousness, for example—may be presented as a range around a mean trajectory, reflecting simulations across the plausible or measured values of a parameter, or as separate simulations.[129]

The NBS cannot be focused on the most shocking and sensational aspects of forecasting, but rather on ranges and trends that are managed and understood. National policy decisions on epidemiology should not be made by so-called experts on CNN or during presidential press conferences, but based on sober and thoughtful review of established data and well-conceived policies and procedures.

Another focus of this goal is to enhance bio-surveillance laboratory operations to "strengthen and promote interoperability." This is an example of a laudable goal for which the NBS simply does not provide any details. There is no explanation of how the federal government can or should strengthen these laboratory operations. It was clear that this did not mean the administration was going to increase funding for these laboratories, given that funding did not increase in the last 2 years. It is hard to believe that funding will not increase as a result of the COVID-19 pandemic.

GOAL 2: Ensure biodefense capabilities to prevent bio-incidents. This goal aims to prevent outbreaks from occurring or to mitigate outbreaks if they occur. The U.S. government intends to prevent or limit the spread of infectious disease. Most of the details of this objective are vague and read like the kind of bureaucratic gibberish that those of us who served in government grew to despise, and that further undermines public confidence in government institutions.

However, some key points have been brought home as a result of the COVID-19 crisis. The NBS emphasizes the limitation of border introduction of biohazards by testing and quarantining people (and animals) from countries of viral outbreak. This was indeed put in place early in the COVID-19 pandemic.

Successful implementation requires cooperation with foreign governments and international organizations, and this was clearly a failure during the COVID-19 crisis. Cooperation requires transparent partners, and there is no doubt that China misled the United States and other countries about the nature and severity of the threat at an early enough date to effectively isolate it. Likewise, the WHO was not candid, whether through negligence or on purpose, with the United States and Europe.

Another objective is to ensure that the United States detects and denies the development and use of biological weapons. Both nation-state and terrorist actors are capable of acquiring such biological weapons, and the goal is to deter those actors and deny the acquisition and use of biological weapons.

This objective also recognizes that the United States is committed to the Biological Weapons Convention (BWC), an international treaty to which it has been a party since the treaty's inception in 1975. It is an almost universal global treaty (183 member states). The BWC establishes the baseline to which all signatories agree: No country will develop biological weapons.

The BWC does not have a compliance mechanism. Although it can ask the UN Security Council to investigate (and presumably implement actions against a state or non-state actor), it has not successfully deterred biological weapons development.

GOAL 3: Ensure biodefense enterprise preparedness to reduce the impacts of bio-incidents. Building and maintaining the capability to respond to biological incidents includes a robust public health system and support for innovative technologies developed by an improved science and technology base.

This is the heart of the National Biodefense Strategy and involves recommendations to develop outbreak containment plans, community measures, communication, veterinary health infrastructure, and preparedness.

While these are worthy goals, the NBS is missing any practical approach to implementing most of these objectives. Given the broad scope of these goals, to take maintaining public health systems and developing community measures as an example, it is not surprising that practical implementation is difficult. Even evaluating the success or failure of such programs would be difficult.

One important objective of this goal is to improve diagnostic capabilities, the importance of which came into vivid focus during the COVID-19 pandemic. The urgent need to develop testing has been one of the primary necessities of the crisis.

The new focus, of course, is on developing a vaccine. It must be noted, however, that the urgent work of testing and vaccine development has been an ad hoc process. The level of cooperation between the federal government and private industry has been impressive and the effort is beyond anything that was anticipated by the NBS.

GOAL 4: Rapidly respond to limit the impacts of bio-incidents. This goal seeks to ensure that in the event of a biological outbreak, whether an attack or a natural disease, the response would be quick enough to limit the scope and duration of the outbreak. This effort would entail two primary elements.

First, there would be an information collection system shared with government agencies and the private sector to ensure that decisions at the federal level would be quick and informed. The NBS's goal is to have real-time information sharing between government agencies and state, local, and foreign governments.

Second, in addition to public health information, intelligence information will be used. This important addition enables all relevant information to be used even if it is initially classified. This is further supported by the designation of the National Security Advisor as the coordinator of policy development, even while the Secretary of Health and Human Services is the chair of the interagency committee.

GOAL 5: Facilitate recovery to restore the community, the economy, and the environment after a bio-incident. Prior to the COVID-19 pandemic, disease outbreaks in the United States had little or no impact on the economy or on the social fabric of the country. To the extent any economic impact from outbreaks occurred, its effect tended to be local. In the 1990s, outbreaks of mad cow disease caused major disruption to the beef industry in the United Kingdom and later in the United States.[130] Some local outbreaks can disrupt tourism and local economies.

COVID-19 has caused the kind of global economic and social disruption only seen in times of war. Only the 1918 influenza pandemic (Spanish Flu) can compare, and even that probably does not exceed what we have seen in 2020.

Modern economies are based on transportation of individuals and goods, and the oil and energy industries that fuel movement. All over the world, and particularly in the United States, transportation has been disrupted, resulting in unemployment, falling GDP, and social disruption.

Recognition of this as a major potential impact of a bio-incident might be the most forward-looking, insightful aspect of the National Biodefense Strategy. This part of the NBS specifically recognizes the need to restore the infrastructure and public health capability after the disruption of a major pandemic or biological attack. It identifies long-term recovery and mitigation actions from a public health perspective as vital to getting a country back to the point where economic and social recovery can succeed.

But the major point—and, appropriately its final objective—is to ensure economic recovery, as the NBS puts it, "to mitigate the second order impacts of a bio-incident."

We have seen this economic disruption in a way that not even the authors of the National Biodefense Strategy could have imagined would hit the United States and the world 2 years later. The NBS itself is, again, short on how we should do this. The two major bills passed during the COVID-19 pandemic surpassed anything the federal government had done before, to the tune of $10 trillion or so.

These bills had to be done on the fly and under extreme circumstances, so there was really no choice but to pass them as they were. But detailed planning could have given Congress and other decision-makers a better understanding of what actions would be likely to put the economy and the society back on its feet, and minimize the potential for waste, fraud, and abuse. Instead, we are taking steps that might be correct or might be unnecessary.

What Now?

The COVID-19 pandemic put the National Biodefense Strategy to the test. The NBS was unable to properly coordinate the nations' response to the pandemic, prompting calls for a complete overhaul of biodefense policy.[131] The requirement to develop a strategy was part of the 2017 National Defense Authorization Act. As any seasoned career government official would recognize, the "Strategy" reads like a group of officials going through the motions of meeting a Congressional mandate, and not like a strategy worthy of the name. There is no attempt to develop programs, fund stockpiles, or equip laboratories. There is just a repetitive 30-page paper that contains some good ideas but no offers no practical implementation. Only a bureaucrat would believe that forming committees is a solution to a problem.

No plan survives first contact with the enemy, as Moltke the Elder stated in the 19th century, so it would be wrong to expect perfection in any strategy. When the COVID-19 pandemic began, the National Biodefense Strategy ceased to be of any use because it wasn't a strategy at all. At best it was a plan to make a plan, but that plan never happened. As always in crisis management, it is the crisis itself that causes plans to be made out of necessity. The COVID-19 crisis is the impetus to move forward with a real strategy. The American public is entitled to it, and foreign adversaries know our vulnerabilities better than they did before. The horrific human cost of this crisis is an opportunity to develop real plans to deal with public health emergencies.

11.

BACK TO THE FUTURE: BIOSECURITY LESSONS FROM THE LATE 1990S FOR THE YEAR OF COVID-19*

By John Lauder

T he assault of COVID-19 on the economy and well-being of the United States, and the health of our citizens, highlights the vulnerability of the country to infectious disease. The current focus on how the United States could have prepared better for a highly contagious virus like COVID-19 was presaged in many ways by efforts to assess and address biological weapons and pandemic disease threats in the 1990s. Much of how the U.S. government views the anticipation and mitigation of biological and public health threats was forged in the 1990s, especially during the latter part of the decade. The views formed then have been reaffirmed and amplified at several key junctures since then and provide a road map for shaping future biodefense strategy.

Five trends and sets of events reinforced each other in the 1990s to create a fertile period for developing measures and strategies to assess and mitigate the vulnerability of the United States to biological attack and by extension to pandemic disease:

- First, the collapse of the Soviet Union gave rise to fear that expertise and material that had been part of that country's extensive Weapons of Mass Destruction (WMD) programs would bleed out to other states and to non-state terrorist groups.

---

* This chapter was reviewed for publication by the CIA Prepublications Classification Review Board who determined that the submission contained no classified information.

- Second, the general concern about the fate of Soviet WMD programs gained a specific biological focus when two prominent defectors who had worked in those programs described the full extent of the threat.

- Third, in the aftermath of the war with Iraq to throw Saddam Hussein's forces out of Kuwait, the international community discovered that the Iraqis had advanced much further in biological weapons programs than previously believed.

- Fourth, the attack by Aum Shinrikyo in the Tokyo Subway System in 1995—combined with a series of conventional terrorist attacks—underscored the vulnerability of the United States to biological weapons attacks.

- Fifth, later in the 1990s, biological threats became part of popular literature and imagination with the publication of books such as *The Cobra Event*.[132]

These five developments combined to create a consensus in the United States that more needed to be done to anticipate and counter biological and public health threats. This consensus extended across both parties, within both the executive and legislative branches of government, through nongovernmental institutions, and into the general public. The common goal to do better led to a series of government programs and outreach efforts. The lessons from those efforts, and the reasons they were not sustained, help illuminate the challenges of dealing with public health issues in this COVID-19 era.

In the 1990s, the world was dealing with the consequences of the Soviet Union's collapse. It was a failed state with enormous capability and expertise in weapons of mass destruction. There was appropriate concern about the security of the former Soviet Union's WMD-related infrastructure, material, facilities, and personnel. Former Soviet scientists and engineers had detailed knowledge of how to build and employ nuclear, chemical, and biological weapons. What was going to happen to this knowledge and to the weapons and precursor materials? Were the expertise and material going to flow out to other states and to non-state actors? How could the relevant facilities be better safeguarded?

As the decade began, concerns about the biological weapons programs of the Soviet Union came further into sharp relief. In 1989 and 1992, two biologists who had been leaders within the Soviet biological weapons program defected to the West. Their reports seemed to corroborate the worst fears in the United States about the sweeping extent and danger of the biological weapons program that was being conducted by the Soviet Union. The revelations came as the U.S. and the Soviet Union had entered an extensive period of arms control negotiations. Within this context, the Soviet biological weapons program became the subject of intense bilateral and trilateral discussions. The United Kingdom, which had been the original recipient of the first defector, was the third party in the talks.[133]

The discussions were conducted initially under great secrecy as the United States did not want to embarrass Russian General Secretary Mikhail Gorbachev or undermine his reform programs. The United States and the United Kingdom sought in the talks to better understand the extent of the Soviet program, to determine how best to dismantle what remained, and to bring the program into arms control or cooperative threat reduction constraints.

The Soviets, and later the Russians, were mostly unenthusiastic participants. In the talks, the Russians first sought to discredit the defectors. They said the defectors had sensationalized their reports, and Moscow admitted to nothing more than what the defectors reported. Russian officials also alleged concerns about U.S. and U.K. biodefense and biological research facilities, claiming that those facilities were part of covert biological weapons programs in the West. There were also a series of visits by U.S. and U.K. experts to facilities associated with the Soviet biological weapons program. The experts had more access to civilian-managed facilities, but did not receive requested access to some facilities of concern, especially those controlled by the military. Nor did the Russians offer a full disclosure of the scope of prior Soviet programs.

Growing awareness of the extent of Iraq's biological weapons program was another shock to the U.S. national security establishment. There had been intelligence reporting that Iraq was pursuing a biological weapons program in the 1990s, and prudent medical precautions were taken against such weapons during the 1991 Gulf War. Still, UN inspections after that war revealed that the international community had badly underestimated Iraqi biological weapons capabilities beforehand.

The Commission on the Intelligence Capabilities of the United States Regarding Weapons of Mass Destruction (WMD Commission or Robb-Silberman Commission) examined intelligence assessments and reporting on the Iraqi BW program both before and after the 1991 Gulf War. The WMD Commission found that it was not until 1995—when the UN Special Commission (the body charged with inspections in Iraq)

> presented the Iraqis with evidence of continuing BW-related imports and Saddam Hussein's son-in-law, Hussein Kamil, defected—that Iraq made substantial declarations to the United Nations about its activities prior to the Gulf War, admitting that it had produced and weaponized BW agents. These declarations confirmed that the Intelligence Community had substantially underestimated the scale and maturity of Iraq's pre-Desert Storm BW program. Iraq had, before the Gulf War, weaponized several agents, including anthrax, botulinum toxin, and aflatoxin.

The WMD Commission also found that Iraq had produced substantial quantities of biological agents and weapons.[134]

Stunned by their failure to divine the broad scope of Iraq's biological weapons activities before 1991, U.S. national security organizations overcorrected in subsequent years and attributed greater BW capability to Iraq than what was maintained. The weaknesses of intelligence collection and analysis of Iraq's BW programs are described in the WMD Commission report. A contributing factor was Saddam's secrecy about his decisions to destroy his stockpiles of biological and chemical weapons after 1991 although he continued to behave as if Iraq had ongoing capabilities. The failure to understand Saddam's actions before and after 1991 equally underscores the intelligence challenges of penetrating covert biological weapons programs.[135]

The newfound awareness of the Soviet and Iraqi biological weapons programs gained greater urgency with a series of terrorist attacks by non-state actors. The most directly relevant to concerns about biological weapons was an attack using nerve agents by Aum Shinrikyo on the Tokyo subway system in March 1995. The Japanese cult group had been experimenting and conducting smaller attacks for years with other biological weapons agents, including anthrax and botulinum toxins.[136]

The 1993 bombing of New York's World Trade Center, the 1995 bombing of the Murrah Federal Building in Oklahoma City, the 1996 attack on the Khobar Towers facility housing deployed U.S. forces in Saudi Arabia, and the bombings of the U.S. embassies in Kenya and Tanzania in August 1998 gave further weight to fears that terrorist groups were motivated, and had the means, to kill in large numbers. There were also reports from the same period that Ramzi Yousef, the mastermind of the World Trade Center bombing, and Osama bin Laden were showing interest in biological and chemical weapons.

In early 1998, President Bill Clinton read *The Cobra Event*, a novel depicting a mad scientist's development and employment of an enhanced and highly contagious biological weapon. The president had a strong interest in the prospect of germ warfare and reached out to discuss his interests and readings with a number of scientists and other experts. One of those scientists, Craig Venter, had recommended the book. Clinton, in turn, encouraged others in and out of government to read it, from House Speaker Newt Gingrich to members of his cabinet. The president wanted to know what the government should do to prevent or prepare for a biological attack, and his interest had a profound effect on government priorities.[137]

In April 1998, a number of leading scientific experts on disease, public health, and biological warfare gathered in the White House along with top government officials. The extended discussion was a watershed moment in the forging of a government-wide strategy and budget increases for biological defense. Joshua Lederberg, a Noble Laureate and one of the nation's most distinguished biologists, reportedly gave President Clinton a copy of a special issue of the *Journal of the American Medical Association*, devoted entirely to the issue of biological weapons. Clinton subsequently circulated that issue among his staff and cabinet to encourage their thinking. Lederberg was said later to be amused that this may have been the only time in U.S. history when a president had read a complete issue of the *JAMA*.[138]

This level of presidential and cabinet attention led to a series of nonproliferation and biodefense initiatives, actions, and programs. A vital element in the strategy and enabling budget was increased attention and funding for the public health system. These programs focused on encouraging greater research on biological issues and on strengthening the range of medical countermeasures available. Other programs were designed to assist the former Soviet states with dismantling and repurposing many of their WMD facilities and to provide support for redirecting their WMD experts to more benign activities. Traditional arms control agreements played a role, as did programs such as the Cooperative Threat Reduction Program and ad hoc efforts such as U.S. visits to former Soviet biological facilities such as the anthrax production facility at Stepnogorsk in Kazakhstan and the VECTOR virology research center in Siberia, where the Soviets had sought to weaponize smallpox.

The U.S. government reorganized itself as well, to bring greater focus and resources to nonproliferation challenges. One of those reorganizations was the creation of the Defense Threat Reduction Agency in 1998, which brought together several elements of the defense department to focus on the WMD problem. Another adjustment was in the intelligence community. A larger nonproliferation center was created in the same year that brought more analysts in from across the community to focus on WMD issues, related technology, and transfer networks. Tom Monath, a leading virologist who had been part of the discussions with the president, was brought in to assist the center as a senior scientist to enhance the Intelligence Community's focus on collection and analysis of biological weapons programs.[139]

These organizational changes were fostered and funded by a bipartisan consensus that reached from the White House to congressional leadership. Senators Sam Nunn, Democrat from Georgia, and Richard Lugar, Republican from Indiana, were the thought leaders and activists in Congress. Early in the decade, Nunn and Lugar had sponsored legislation that provided funding to assist Russia and other former Soviet states in dismantling and securing their nuclear weapons establishment and repurposing the work of the scientists and engineers who had critical knowledge of nuclear weapons design and fabrication. Within a few years, the Nunn-Lugar cooperative programs were expanded to address the former Soviet biological programs.

Then-House of Representatives Speaker Newt Gingrich, who was concerned about the Clinton administration's harvesting of a "peace dividend" by cutting defense and intelligence programs, advanced other legislation to restore funding for intelligence efforts especially related to WMD programs. In late 1998, Gingrich pushed through a large supplemental increase in the intelligence budget that in part was directed toward enhancing collection and analysis related to biological weapons programs.

One of the leaders of the bipartisan effort was Sidney Drell, a renowned nuclear physicist who was an advisor to the government on national security issues. Drell was a leading member of the President's Foreign Intelligence Advisory Panel and used that position, in the words of one former senior intelligence official, to prod the government "relentlessly to improve" its performance on nonproliferation, including efforts to assess and address the biological weapons threat. Drell was a principal organizer of a seminal conference on biological and chemical weapons at the Hoover Institution at Stanford University in November 1998. The event brought together leaders across science, medicine, law, intelligence, defense, law enforcement, and public health.[140]

The conference surveyed and outlined further steps to counter biological weapons in five domains: intelligence enhancements, scientific research, international norms and monitoring, consequence management, and defensive measures, including deterrence. An important component of the consequence management discussion at the conference was the need to strengthen public health, including by increasing stocks of antivirals, antibiotics, and vaccines and expanding research and production capability for new drugs. One speaker specifically identified ventilators as an example of critical medical equipment that would be needed "to treat patients suffering from chemical or biological agent exposure. Each city or region cannot fund the development of a cache of ventilators individually; a national, mobile supply is essential."[141]

The major purposes of the Hoover Institution Conference were to increase public attention to biological threats and to broaden the amount of information for public discourse. The conference organizers did this by inviting notable speakers to present, including former Secretary of State George Shultz, Navy Secretary Richard Danzig, former Executive Chairman of the United Nations Special Commission Rolf Ekeus, and then-Stanford Provost Condoleezza Rice. Media attention was encouraged both at the conference and to cover later developments in biosecurity.

For example, the Intelligence Community did a series of press briefings over the next few years and even made the head of the CIA Nonproliferation Center available for on-camera interviews for a series on the history of chemical and biological warfare that first appeared on the History Channel in May 2001.[142]

In a related outreach effort, John Gannon, the chairman of the National Intelligence Council at the time and a keynote speaker at the Stanford Conference, commissioned a series of unclassified intelligence assessments that addressed global health issues. One of the first was a National Intelligence Estimate, *The Global Infectious Disease Threat and Its Implications for the United States.* The first sentence of the key judgments of this report now seems prescient: "New and reemerging infectious diseases will pose a rising global health threat and will complicate US and global security over the next 20 years."[143]

Over time, though, public and congressional attention and the commitment of government agencies to the mitigation of biological threats declined. No major biological attacks or public health crises were endured. There was too much else on the plate of important domestic and international issues and a vast range of other demands for scarce resources. Indeed, one of the challenges that was confronted in the late 1990s was the tremendous scope of issues for the new nonproliferation and biosecurity organizations and programs to address. How should these organizations, and the United States government as a whole, prioritize the most dangerous threats and what needed to be done to confront them? Some officials used the phrase *the sum of all fears* to summarize the range of WMD threats faced by the United States.[144] They sought to devise a method for the government to rack and stack the sum of all proliferation, terrorism, and WMD fears, and use that sum of assessments to assign priorities and allocate scarce resources. This was a noble idea, but it proved difficult to implement—largely because the range of threats was broad and perception of the imminence of the threats was affected by so many factors inside and outside the government.

Those priorities, and the associated feast and famine of government budgeting, were shaped by external events. Most dramatic were the terrorist actions on 9/11. Those attacks underscored that terrorists could create a tremendous catastrophe even without the use of WMD. At the same time, 9/11 raised the specter of ever more spectacular terrorist assaults that could possibly employ WMD, including biological weapons. The anthrax letter attacks and copycat hoaxes later in 2001 gave further emphasis to biological defense measures.

In the wake of these concerns, there were renewed efforts to come up with the sum of all fears and prioritize the threats. One related analytical effort was the Defense Science Board Summer Study of 2005 on *Reducing Vulnerabilities to Weapons of Mass Destruction*.[145] Members of the study team and the Defense Science Board as a whole included some who had been instrumental in shaping biosecurity initiatives in the late 1990s.

Only a few years removed from 9/11 and the subsequent anthrax scare, the Summer Study aimed to examine threats across the broad range of possible WMD attacks. The study considered state actors' use of WMD across the full modalities of chemical, biological, radiological, and nuclear. The report addressed state-sponsored terrorism and the possibility that states might use WMD against the United States in nonconventional ways, such as using special operations forces to introduce a weapon into a city rather than using a missile or air strike. The study also looked at the possibility of non-state actors developing a crude WMD device.

The study did not just consider a single use, but examined what would happen if a series of attacks took place or attackers combined different modalities of weaponry. For example, what if there was a cyberattack that degraded response capabilities at the same time that a terrorist group employed a biological or nuclear weapon?

A striking aspect of the timing of that Defense Science Board report was that Hurricane Katrina struck the U.S. Gulf Coast at the end of that summer. One focus of the study had been to assess the ability of the U.S. government to do effective and well-coordinated consequence management in the wake of a truly catastrophic event. The study team had received a number of briefings from government agencies about how federal, state, tribal, and local governments would cooperate to respond to a catastrophe; the right resources would be requested promptly, arrive on time, and be effectively employed.

There was much skepticism on the part of the study team that the necessary operational plans were in place. The team doubted there had been sufficient exercising and detailed planning of how to work together to respond to a catastrophe—how the handoffs would occur among local first responders, state resources, federal civilian agencies, and ultimately the U.S. military if required. Unfortunately, those concerns turned out to be well-placed when the response to Katrina exposed failures in catastrophe planning and preparation.

The team looked at biological terrorism in the same context. In the course of the study, the team came to focus on the bookend of, on one side, prevention—how do you stop an event from happening? On the other end was consequence management—how can you prepare to mitigate and recover? How could the resources and planning of the public health system be improved to deal with both major epidemics and possible biological attacks?

Several of the report's findings and recommendations have direct relevance to the COVID-19 crisis. The study found that the nation is "still poorly prepared" to deal with a WMD terrorist attack and, by extension, a public health emergency. The lack of preparation appears

> to result from several key factors: fuzzy lines of responsibility and authority among local, state, and federal agencies involved; a lack of a sense of urgency; and a tendency to emphasize physical effects of an attack with little regard for the psychological.

The study recommended "radically increasing medical surge capabilities." It also suggested the best way to publicly articulate the situation during a crisis. The president and other senior officials should communicate "clearly and honestly, with realistic assessments and guidance, to gain and maintain public support and to increase the sense of urgency."[146]

The study team was particularly worried that, in addition to the sheer destruction and casualties, a catastrophic attack would fundamentally weaken the U.S. economy and undermine confidence in government. What would be the economic impact of losing the financial centers of lower Manhattan to an attack, especially if other attacks also took place or were threatened? What would be the impact on democracy as we know it?

The concern was that economic and political upheavals following a major WMD attack in the United States would be much more severe and dramatic than 9/11. The public would demand moves toward a much more authoritarian state to deal with the consequences and the possibility of further attacks. Such an attack may not be likely, but the consequences would be so severe that actions are required to prevent it from happening and to plan to mitigate the impact on the country's health, economy, and society.

We should not be comforted that biological attacks have not happened as was feared in the 1990s and later. One can argue that counterproliferation and counterterrorism actions and programs are working. A more pessimistic assessment is that we are living on borrowed time. No domestic WMD attack has happened in the last decade, and no WMD attacks occurred overseas except for chemical weapons use in Syria. Yet, such attacks could be right around the corner. The COVID-19 crisis demonstrates how vulnerable modern societies and economies are to pandemic diseases, whether naturally occurring or manmade.

In the nearly 22 years since the 1998 Security Forum at the Hoover Institution and the 15 years since the publication of the 2005 DSB Summer Study, the attention of the U.S. government and the public on biological security issues has waxed and waned. It is beyond the scope of this chapter to try to assess or describe the many efforts related to biosecurity in more recent years. As it was in the 1990s and early 2000s, though, it has been hard to sustain attention on those issues for several reasons. The attention span on any national security issue is short. The focus of policymakers is driven by the tyranny of their inbox and their obligation to deal with current crises. Most recognize the importance of long-term planning and investment, but it is difficult to devote scarce resources of time and money when there are more immediate needs than available resources. Hence, the country has gone through a series of feasts and famines in its commitment to dealing with biological threats.

There are lessons from the efforts of the 1990s and early 2000s that have again been illuminated by the COVID-19 crisis. Construction, execution, and sustenance of effective biosecurity programs, and the public health capacity needed to enable such programs and to prevail in a crisis, require several ingredients.

- **Presidential leadership is key.** Government bureaucracies and budget overseers pay attention to what the president believes is important. President Clinton's attention to biological issues, especially after reading *The Cobra Event*, and President George W. Bush's attention to interdicting the spread of weapons of mass destruction in the wake of the 9/11 attacks, galvanized government action.

- **Effective action requires bipartisan executive and legislative support and a whole-of-government approach.** The full range of tools to prevent biological attacks and to prepare the nation's first responders and public health infrastructure do not come cheaply and without controversy. Fostering a bipartisan consensus can help ease the political pain and marshal the resources. These tasks are beyond the scope of any one agency or organization, so sustained leadership from the top is required. It remains to be seen who on Capitol Hill can step up to provide that leadership now that figures such as Nunn and Lugar, who helped enable the biodefense programs of the 1990s, are no longer there.

- **The nature of biological threats also requires strong public–private partnerships.** A remarkable aspect of the prior successes in building strong biodefense programs was the strong degree to which the leading scientists of the day from outside government were energetically and publicly engaged. Those scientists were instrumental in shaping the strategy and building support for it both within and outside government. The marshaling of good science and the innovation of the private sector are vital to successful and cost-effective biodefense programs.

- **International data sharing and information disclosures are vital.** The lack of full disclosure by Russia of the extent and details of the Soviet Union's biological weapons programs hampered understanding of the potential scope and direction of future biological threats. The lack of Iraqi candor about its biological programs in the wake of the first Gulf War helped fuel overestimates of the extent of its programs. And Chinese unwillingness to be forthcoming about the origins of COVID-19 are even today frustrating international response.

- **Transparency and credibility with the public help build support and are essential for crisis management.** The American public is an essential partner in effective biodefense. Public understanding of the threats and the corresponding need to commit substantial resources are critical for programs to be built and carried out in a democracy. The public also needs to believe that the country's political leadership is telling it like it is. The public outreach efforts of the late 1990s concerning the need for biodefense programs—such as expressed during the Stanford conference and the recommendations of the Defense Science Board for candor and honesty in government statements during a crisis—had the goal of building credibility and trust.

Biological terrorism or state-sponsored biological attacks may not be perceived as a near-term urgency, but, as the widespread disruption caused by COVID-19 shows, the consequences of missing warning signs would be enormous. Prudent steps can be taken to assess the risk, even in a time of limited resources and other pressing priorities. We can assess how well the government is implementing recommendations like those of the Defense Science Board. Which recommendations have been implemented, which are still valid, which ones could still be done, and what further innovation is required?

There are other steps as well: strengthening intelligence, fostering international cooperation, exercising consequence management for a catastrophic event, developing more effective attribution and deterrence policies, and being ever more vigilant about reducing and safeguarding stockpiles and production of dangerous biological material. The key is to remain focused on the problem of biological defense. The experience of dealing with COVID-19 underscores the enormous economic and societal costs of a major public health emergency. Steps taken now would be much more effective—and far less costly—than waiting for a biological attack.

The scientists cited earlier in this article had a saying: "The germs always win." They were referring to the near-constant mutations of dangerous organisms to find a way to survive despite the best efforts of modern medicine to counter them. Josh Lederberg himself is quoted as saying "The single biggest threat to man's continued dominance on the planet is the virus." But mankind too is adaptable. We can innovate and organize to defeat even the most persistent natural or manmade organism. The biodefense plans formulated in the 1990s show us paths to do so.

ABOUT THE AUTHORS

FRED FLEITZ is the president and CEO of the Center for Security Policy. He served in 2018 as a deputy assistant to President Donald Trump and National Security Council Executive Secretary. He previously served in U.S. national security positions for 25 years with the CIA, the DIA Armed Forces Medical Intelligence Center, the Department of State, and the House Intelligence Committee staff. He is the author or editor of seven books on national security, including *Growing Challenges for America's Nuclear Deterrent*, published in February 2020.

DR. KEN ALIBEK is a former research director of the Soviet Union's biological weapons program. He is an expert in the field of biological weapons and biodefense, acute and chronic infections, microbiology, and virology. He is the author of more than 60 articles in American and international peer-reviewed journals and has written and edited six monographs, including the bestseller *Biohazard: The Chilling True Story of the Largest Covert Biological Weapons Program in the World—Told from Inside by the Man Who Ran It*. He was awarded the bronze medal by the U.S. Congress "For the Recognition of Outstanding Contributions to World Peace." Alibek consulted for the Government of Singapore on defense against SARS-CoV in 2003–2004.

DR. STEPHEN BRYEN has more than 40 years of experience in government and industry. He served in government as a senior staff director of the U.S. Senate Foreign Relations Committee, Deputy Under Secretary of Defense for Trade Security Policy, founder and first director of the Defense Technology Security Administration, and as a Commissioner of the U.S.–China Security Review Commission. He was twice the recipient of the Defense Department's highest civilian award. In industry, Dr. Bryen was president of Delta Tech Inc. and president of Finmeccanica North America. He is the author of *Technology Security and National Power: Winners and Losers: Essays in Technology, Security and Strategy* and *Security for Holy Places*.

SHOSHANA BRYEN is senior director of the Jewish Policy Center and editor of *inFOCUS Quarterly*. She was previously executive director and senior director for security policy at JINSA. She has worked with the Strategic Studies Institute of the U.S. Army War College and the Institute for National Security Studies in Tel Aviv, and lectured at the National Defense University. Mrs. Bryen coordinated programs that allowed hundreds of American military professionals to engage in discussion with their counterparts in Israel and Jordan. She also created a program to take the cadets and midshipmen of America's service academies to Israel, permitting hundreds of future officers to have a positive, in-depth experience in the Jewish State.

GORDON G. CHANG lived and worked in Asia for almost two decades. He is the author of *The Coming Collapse of China*, *Nuclear Showdown: North Korea Takes on the World* and *Losing South Korea*. His writings on China and North Korea have appeared in the *New York Times*, the *Wall Street Journal*, *Commentary*, *National Review*, *National Interest*, and *Barron's*. Chang has given numerous briefings in Washington and other capitals and frequently appears on CNN, Fox News Channel, Fox Business Network, Bloomberg, CNBC, MSNBC, and PBS.

PAULA A. DESUTTER is an independent consultant who served as assistant secretary for the Department of State for the Bureau of Verification and Compliance from 2002 to 2009. Ms. DeSutter has an extensive background in verification, national security, and intelligence. She served for over 4 years as a professional staff member of the U.S. Senate Select Committee on Intelligence (SSCI). Prior to her work on the SSCI, she worked at the Arms Control & Disarmament Agency on verification and compliance assessments. Ms. DeSutter's publications include *Denial and Jeopardy: Deterring Iranian Use of NBC Weapons* (NDU Press, 1998).

STEPHEN A. ELLIOTT is a lawyer, businessman, and diplomat with decades of experience in the practice of law and compliance with international agreements. He presently serves as general counsel of IAI North America. Prior to joining the private sector in 2012, Mr. Elliott served for 17 years in various positions in the Defense and State Departments. In 2007, Secretary of State Condoleezza Rice appointed

Mr. Elliott as Principal Deputy Assistant Secretary of State for Compliance. In that position, he oversaw the analysis of compliance with Weapons of Mass Destruction agreements, including the Biological Weapons Convention.

CHARLES "SAM" FADDIS is a retired Army captain, a retired CIA operations officer, a senior partner with Artemis LLC, a published author, and the senior editor for *AND Magazine*. Sam took the first CIA team into Iraq approximately a year in advance of the 2003 invasion and retired as the head of the CIA's WMD terrorism unit. Sam is a frequent contributor to the *Washington Times*, *The Hill*, *Newsmax* and *Magazine*. Sam has a B.A. from Johns Hopkins University and a J.D. from the University of Maryland School of Law. His books include *Beyond Repair: The Rise and Fall of the CIA*, *Willful Neglect: The Dangerous Illusion of Homeland Security* and *The CIA War in Kurdistan*.

JIM GERAGHTY, *National Review*'s senior political correspondent, was named CPAC's Journalist of the Year in 2015 and also won the Young Conservatives Coalition's William F. Buckley award that year. He writes the *Morning Jolt* newsletter and contributes to NRO's *Corner* blog. He's the author of *Heavy Lifting* with Cam Edwards, the novel *The Weed Agency* (a Washington Post bestseller) and *Voting to Kill*. Geraghty appears regularly on CNN's *At This Hour* and Fox News' *MediaBuzz* as well as other cable news programs. His reporting has appeared in the *Washington Post*, *Boston Globe*, *Denver Post*, *Detroit Free Press*, *Bergen Record*, *Dallas Morning News*, and *Congressional Quarterly*, and the now-departed websites *Policy.com* and *IntellectualCapital.com*.

ROSEMARY GIBSON is senior advisor at the Hastings Center and author of *China Rx: Exposing the Risks of America's Dependence on China for Medicine*, which reveals the dramatic shift in where medicines are made and growing concerns about their safety. It highlights the centralization of the global supply of medicines in a single country and the implications of that centralization in a global pandemic, natural disaster, or geopolitical event. Ms. Gibson has testified before the House and Senate and to the U.S.–China Economic and Security Review Commission, and briefs leaders in government and industry on national security threats and risk mitigation.

JOHN A. LAUDER is an independent consultant on weapons of mass destruction, nonproliferation, arms control, and intelligence. He retired from the U.S. government with over 33 years of managerial, analytical, and policy experience in the Central Intelligence Agency and National Reconnaissance Office and as an arms control negotiator. He served subsequently as a senior manager and corporate officer within Arete' Associates. Mr. Lauder continues to be instrumental in shaping research and strategic planning in the public and private sectors, including as a member of government, academic, and laboratory advisory panels. Mr. Lauder has received multiple awards for his leadership and innovation in collection systems, analytical approaches, and vital national security initiatives and decisions. He has a B.A. summa cum laude from Hiram College and an M.A. in international relations from Yale University.

CLAUDIA ROSETT is a foreign policy fellow with the Independent Women's Forum and an award-winning journalist who has reported over the past 37 years from Asia, the former Soviet Union, Latin America, and the Middle East. She also is a former *Wall Street Journal* staff writer and blogs at *The Rosett Report* at PJ Media.

ALBINA TSKHAY is the leader of the scientific and analytical group evaluating the effectiveness of treatment methods and developing new biomedical products at Locus Fermentation Solutions. She is one of the leading authors of seven scientific articles written for peer-reviewed journals in the United States on the role of infections in the development of neurological, oncological, and other diseases. She also is the author of 22 patents and patent applications and the author of the concept of new antimicrobial drugs of biological origin for the creation of new disinfectants. She participated in a large number of studies responsible for the development and use of methods with Dr. Ken Alibek, using methods of statistical and bioinformatics analysis. She studied microbiology at the University of Florida.

ENDNOTES

[1] Everett, B. (2020, April 29). The GOP's no. 1 coronavirus China hawk. *Politico.* https://www.politico.com/news/2020/04/29/tom-cotton-china-215230

[2] Wuhan Institute of Virology. *Recruitment page.* http://www.whiov.cas.cn/105341/

[3] Geraghty, Jim. (2020, March 23). The comprehensive timeline of China's COVID-19 lies. *National Review Online.* https://www.nationalreview.com/the-morning-jolt/chinas-devastating-lies/

[4] Zuo, M., Cheng, L., Yan, A., & Yau, C. (2019, December 31). Hong Kong takes emergency measures as mystery "pneumonia" infects dozens in China's Wuhan city. *South China Morning Post.*

[5] Qiu, J. (2020, June). How China's "bat woman" hunted down viruses from SARS to the new coronavirus. *Scientific American.* https://www.scientificamerican.com/article/how-chinas-bat-woman-hunted-down-viruses-from-sars-to-the-new-coronavirus1/ (Reprinted from "Chasing plagues," *Scientific American, 322*(6), 24–32. https://doi.org/10.1038/scientificamerican0620-24)

[6] Kormann, C. (2020, March 27). From bats to human lungs: The evolution of a coronavirus. *The New Yorker.* https://www.newyorker.com/science/elements/from-bats-to-human-lungs-the-evolution-of-a-coronavirus

[7] Wang, M., Cao, R., Zhang, L., Yang, X., Liu, J., Xu, M., Shi, Z., Hu, Z., Zhong, W., & Xiao, G. (2020). Remdesivir and chloroquine effectively inhibit the recently emerged novel coronavirus (2019-nCoV) in vitro. *Cell Research, 30*, 269–271. https://doi.org/10.1038/s41422-020-0282-0

[8] Mai, J. (2020, February 16). "Chinese research lab denies rumours of links to first coronavirus patient. *South China Morning Post.*

[9] Ma, J. (2020, March 13). Coronavirus: China's first confirmed Covid-19 case traced back to November 17. *South China Morning Post.*

[10] Xinjua, P. (2020, February 23). *Rumors stop with the wise.* China Global Television Network. https://news.cgtn.com/news/2020-02-23/Rumors-stop-with-the-wise-OjMaO0RjGM/index.html

[11] Archived images of these pages can be found at Xiao, B., & Xiao, L., (2020), *The possible origins of 2019-nCoV coronavirus*, Wayback Machine, https://web.archive.org/web/20200214144447/https:/www.researchgate.net/publication/339070128_The_possible_origins_of_2019-nCoV_coronavirus; and at Durden, T., (2020, February 15), *Smoking gun? Chinese scientist finds "Killer coronavirus probably originated from a laboratory in Wuhan,"* ZeroHedge,

https://www.zerohedge.com/health/smoking-gun-chinese-scientist-finds-killer-coronavirus-probably-originated-laboratory-wuhan

[12] Camero, K. (2020, February 6). Scientists link China coronavirus to intersection of humans and wildlife, *Wall Street Journal*, https://www.wsj.com/articles/scientists-link-china-virus-to-intersection-of-humans-and-wildlife-11580997600

[13] Areddy, J. T. (2020, March 5). Coronavirus epidemic draws scrutiny to labs handling deadly pathogens. *Wall Street Journal*. https://www.wsj.com/articles/coronavirus-epidemic-draws-scrutiny-to-labs-handling-deadly-pathogens-11583349777

[14] Jqknews.com. (2020, February 23). *Latest overseas research: bats carrying new coronavirus may directly infect people.* https://www.jqknews.com/news/393098-Latest_overseas_research_bats_carrying_new_coronavirus_may_directly_infect_people.html

[15] Sanders, R. (2020, February 10). *Coronavirus outbreak raises question: Why are bat viruses so deadly?* Berkeley News. https://news.berkeley.edu/2020/02/10/coronavirus-outbreak-raises-question-why-are-bat-viruses-so-deadly/

[16] Bryner, J. (2020, March 21). *The coronavirus was not engineered in a lab. Here's how we know.* LiveScience. https://www.livescience.com/coronavirus-not-human-made-in-lab.html

[17] Kline, F. (2020, March 26). *Genomic study points to natural origin of COVID-19.* NIH Director's Blog. https://directorsblog.nih.gov/2020/03/26/genomic-research-points-to-natural-origin-of-covid-19/

[18] Tiankai, C. (2020, April 5). China and the U.S. must cooperate against coronavirus. *New York Times.* https://www.nytimes.com/2020/04/05/opinion/coronavirus-china-us.html.

[19] Areddy, J. T. (2020, May 26).China rules out animal market and lab as coronavirus origin. *Wall Street Journal.* https://www.wsj.com/articles/china-rules-out-animal-market-and-lab-as-coronavirus-origin-11590517508. Beijing now maintains that a wet market in Wuhan was not the source of the coronavirus. By systematically ruling out Chinese sources, it appears to be making the case that the disease began elsewhere.

[20] Chen, S. (2020, April 17). Coronavirus outbreak may have started in September, say British scientists. *South China Morning Post* (Hong Kong). https://www.scmp.com/news/china/science/article/3080380/coronavirus-outbreak-may-have-started-september-say-british

[21] Global Times. (2020, May 18). *Full text: Chinese President Xi Jinping delivers speech at WHA session opening ceremony.* https://www.globaltimes.cn/content/1188716.shtml. Xi's call was in line with

the Chinese Foreign Ministry's position on the subject. In early May, for instance, the ministry announced it supported the WHO establishing a "review committee" to evaluate global responses to COVID-19 "at an appropriate time after the pandemic is over." See Ministry of Foreign Affairs of the People's Republic of China, (2020, May 8), Foreign Ministry Spokesperson Hua Chunying's regular press conference on May 8, 2020, https://www.fmprc.gov.cn/mfa_eng/xwfw_665399/s2510_665401/t1777215.s html. For more, see Jin, Z., (2020, May 9), Nation backs WHO on new committee, *China Daily* (Beijing). http://global.chinadaily.com.cn/a/202005/09/WS5eb5fdb6a310a8b2411545fa. html.

[22] Page, J., & Khan, N. (2020, May 12). China stalls the global search for coronavirus origins. *Wall Street Journal*. https://www.wsj.com/articles/china-stalls-global-search-for-coronavirus-origins-wuhan-markets-investigation-11589300842. Chen Xu, China's ambassador to the United Nations in Geneva, said on May 6 that Beijing would reject any investigation by researchers while the coronavirus was still spreading around the world and while Washington was making accusations against Beijing. See Li, G., (2020, May 6), *China refuses international investigation on origin of virus*, Radio France Internationale.

[23] World Health Organization. (2020, January 22). *Mission summary: WHO field visit to Wuhan, China 20–21 January 2020.* https://www.who.int/china/news/detail/22-01-2020-field-visit-wuhan-china-jan-2020.

[24] Pinghui, Z. (2020, May 15). China confirms unauthorized labs were told to destroy early coronavirus samples. *South China Morning Post* (Hong Kong). https://www.scmp.com/news/china/society/article/3084635/china-confirms-unauthorised-labs-were-told-destroy-early.

[25] World Health Organization. (2020, February 25). *WHO emergencies coronavirus press conference—Dr. Bruce Aylward.* https://www.who.int/docs/default-source/coronaviruse/who-audio-emergencies-coronavirus-press-conference-aylwardb-25feb2020-final.pdf?sfvrsn=9d732ce3_0

[26] World Health Organization. (2020, February 28). *Report of the WHO-China joint mission on coronavirus disease 2019 (COVID-19).* https://www.who.int/publications-detail/report-of-the-who-china-joint-mission-on-coronavirus-disease-2019-(covid-19).

[27] Simmons, C. (2020, June 1). The WHO Has a Confession to Make: Investigations on Chinese Wet Markets or Labs Never Took Place. ScienceTimes.com. https://www.sciencetimes.com/articles/25894/20200601/who-confession-make-investigations-chinese-wet-markets-labs-never-took.htm.

[28] Sean Lin, X. (2020, May 11). Email message to author.

[29] See note 26.

[30] See note 28.

[31] See Page and Khan, note 23.

[32] Azar, A. M. II. (2020, January 28). *Remarks at coronavirus press briefing.* U.S. Department of Health & Human Services. https://www.hhs.gov/about/leadership/secretary/speeches/2020-speeches/remarks-at-coronavirus-press-briefing.html.

[33] See note 23.

[34] China deliberately destroyed and concealed evidence relating to the COVID-19 outbreak according to a leaked "Five Eyes" report. See Shaw, A., Turner, G., & Roberts, J., (2020, May 2), *Leaked "Five Eyes" dossier on alleged Chinese coronavirus coverup consistent with US findings, officials say,* Fox News, https://www.foxnews.com/politics/five-eyes-dossier-chinese-coronavirus-coverup-u-s-findings. For more information on Beijing's attempts to hide information, see Gertz, B., (2020, April 4), Thanks for nothing: U.S. scientists say China hampering search for virus origin, *Washington Times.*

[35] See Page and Khan, note 23.

[36] State Council Information Office of People's Republic of China. (2020, June). Fighting COVID-19: China in Action. http://www.xinhuanet.com/english/2020-06/07/c_139120424.htm.

[37] Betz, B. (2020, May 13). *China has arrested hundreds for speaking out about coronavirus, reports show.* Fox News. https://www.foxnews.com/world/china-arrested-hundreds-speaking-out-coronavirus.

[38] Wang, V., Qin, A., & Wee, S.-L. (2020, May 5). Coronavirus survivors want answers, and China is silencing them. *New York Times.* https://www.nytimes.com/2020/05/04/world/asia/china-coronavirus-answers.html

[39] Dotson, J. (2020, February 5). *The CCP's new leading small group for countering the coronavirus epidemic—and the mysterious absence of Xi Jinping.* China Brief. The Jamestown Foundation. https://jamestown.org/program/the-ccps-new-leading-small-group-for-countering-the-coronavirus-epidemic-and-the-mysterious-absence-of-xi-jinping/?w3tc_note=flush_all&mc_cid=c40bcd0079&mc_eid=e6543ed168

[40] See Nsoesie, E.O., Rader, B, Barnoon, L., Goodwin, L. & Brownstein, J. (2020, June). Analysis of Hospital Traffic and Search Engine Data in Wuhan China Indicates Early Disease Activity in the Fall of 2019. https://dash.harvard.edu/handle/1/42669767.

[41] World Health Organization, (2020, April 13), COVID-19 Virtual Press Conference [transcript], https://www.who.int/docs/default-source/coronaviruse/transcripts/who-audio-emergencies-coronavirus-press-conference-13apr2020.pdf?sfvrsn=3d574d9e_2

[42] Page, J., Fan, W., & Khan, N. (2020, March 6). How it all started: China's early coronavirus missteps. *Wall Street Journal.* https://www.wsj.com/articles/how-it-all-started-chinas-early-coronavirus-missteps-11583508932

[43] See note 42. The WHO first learned of the coronavirus outbreak on December 31, not from China but from an open-source platform. See also Associated Press, (2020, June 2), China delayed releasing coronavirus info, frustrating WHO, https://apnews.com/3c061794970661042b18d5aeaaed9fae

[44] Chin, J. (2020, May 16). China told labs to destroy coronavirus samples to reduce biosafety risks. *Wall Street Journal.* https://www.wsj.com/articles/china-told-labs-to-destroy-coronavirus-samples-to-reduce-biosafety-risks-11589684291·

[45] Xiaodong, W. (2020, January 21). Top expert: Disease spread won't be on scale of SARS. *China Daily* (Beijing). https://www.chinadaily.com.cn/a/202001/21/WS5e25f635a31012821727256a.html

[46] Fifield, A., & Sun, L. H. (2020, January 23). Chinese cities cancel new year celebrations, travel ban widens in effort to stop coronavirus outbreak. *Washington Post.*

[47] Moore, M. (2020, May 10). China pressured WHO to delay global coronavirus warning: Report. *New York Post.* https://nypost.com/2020/05/10/china-pressured-who-to-delay-global-coronavirus-warning/?utm_campaign=iphone_nyp&utm_source=mail_app·

[48] Jamali, N. & O'Connor, T. (2020, May 12). Exclusive: As China hoarded medical supplies, the CIA believes it tried to stop the WHO from sounding the alarm on the pandemic. *Newsweek.* https://www.newsweek.com/exclusive-cia-believes-china-tried-stop-who-alarm-pandemic-1503565. The U.S. Department of Homeland Security charged in a report that China tried to deceive the world in order to hoard medical supplies. See Weissert, W., (2020, May 4), *DHS Report: China hid virus' severity to hoard supplies,* Associated Press, https://apnews.com/bf685dcf52125be54e030834ab7062a8

[49] McGregor, G. (2020, March 4). China scoffed at being subject to early coronavirus travel restrictions. Now it's enacting its own. *Fortune.* https://fortune.com/2020/03/04/china-coronavirus-travel-restrictions/

[50] Delaney, R. (2020, March 26). Coronavirus: China to ban most foreign arrivals in effort to block contagion's spread. *South China Morning Post* (Hong Kong). https://www.scmp.com/news/china/article/3077175/coronavirus-china-suspend-most-foreign-arrivals-block-contagion-spread·

[51] See note 42.

[52] Rosenbaum, L. (2020, April 7). Wuhan lockdown finally ends after 76 days; Officials alert for second wave of infections. *Forbes.*

https://www.forbes.com/sites/leahrosenbaum/2020/04/07/wuhan-lockdown-finally-ends-after-76-days-officials-alert-for-second-wave-of-infections/#3fb6aa3821e3

[53] Bhatia, G. (2020, February 14). Under China's lockdown, millions have nowhere to go. *Reuters*, https://graphics.reuters.com/CHINA-HEALTH-LOCKDOWN/0100B5EF3LJ/index.html

[54] See note 36.

[55] See Associated Press, note 43. The Associated Press also reported that the National Health Commission's directive also prohibited the Wuhan Institute of Virology from issuing warnings about the disease.

[56] See note 42.

[57] See Pinghui, Z. (2020, February 28). Chinese laboratory that first shared coronavirus genome with world ordered to close for "rectification," hindering its COVID-19 research. *South China Morning Post* (Hong Kong).

[58] See Associated Press, note 43.

[59] See note 58.

[60] Nedelman, M. (2020, January 23). Wuhan coronavirus is not yet a public health emergency of international concern, WHO says. CNN. https://www.cnn.com/2020/01/23/health/who-wuhan-coronavirus-bn/index.html

[61] Wadhams, N. & Jacobs, J. (2020, April 1). China Concealed Extent of Virus Outbreak, U.S. Intelligence Says. Bloomberg News. https://www.bloomberg.com/news/articles/2020-04-01/china-concealed-extent-of-virus-outbreak-u-s-intelligence-says.

[62] Mouton, C., Hanson, R., Grissom, A. & Godges, P. (2020) COVID-19 Air Traffic Visualization: COVID-19 Cases in China Were Likely 37 Times Higher Than Reported in January 2020. RAND Corporation. https://www.rand.org/pubs/research_reports/RRA248-3.html.

[63] Garcia, V. (2020, April 11). *Dr. Fauci: We'll "take a look" at China's handling of coronavirus "when this is all over."* Fox News. https://www.foxnews.com/media/anthony-fauci-china-misinformation-coronavirus-pandemic-watters-world

[64] Fish, I. S., & Sinclair, M. K. (2020, May 12). Leaked Chinese virus database covers 230 cities, 640,000 updates. *Foreign Policy*. https://foreignpolicy.com/2020/05/12/leaked-chinese-coronavirus-database-number-cases/. For an analysis stemming from another leak of Chinese records, see Griffith, C., (2020, May 9), Coronavirus: Hacked Wuhan lab records show unreported cases in wider area, *Australian* (Sydney), https://www.theaustralian.com.au/.

[65] Bloomberg News. (2020, March 27). *Urns in Wuhan prompt new questions of virus's toll.* https://www.bloomberg.com/news/articles/2020-03-27/stacks-of-urns-in-wuhan-prompt-new-questions-of-virus-s-toll. China engaged in many deceptive techniques to hide coronavirus infections and deaths, including constantly changing the method of counting COVID-19 cases and counting asymptomatic cases separately. Moreover, in the beginning of the epidemic, hospitals turned away those with symptoms and did not count those with "lung infections" as coronavirus patients. They did not test lung-infection patients for coronavirus, and authorities cremated corpses quickly. For more on China's deception, see Fan, W. (2020, January 24), Relatives wonder why pneumonia deaths not in coronavirus tally, *Wall Street Journal*, https://www.wsj.com/articles/relatives-wonder-whether-pneumonia-deaths-were-tied-to-coronavirus-11579915630.

[66] Osnos, E. (2020, May 10). The folly of Trump's blame-Beijing coronavirus strategy. *The New Yorker.* https://www.newyorker.com/magazine/2020/05/18/the-folly-of-trumps-blame-beijing-coronavirus-strategy

[67] Cell phone data shows no calls were made from the Wuhan Institute of Virology during an extended period, an indication there was a "hazardous event" between October 6 and 11, 2019. See Dilanian, K., Arrow, R., Kube, C., Lee, C. E., Jones, L., & Bodo, L., (2020, May 8), *Report says cellphone data suggests October shutdown at Wuhan lab, but experts are skeptical*, NBC News, https://www.nbcnews.com/politics/national-security/report-says-cellphone-data-suggests-october-shutdown-wuhan-lab-experts-n1202716. For more evidence of a lab leak, see Hamilton, C. (2020, May 9), It would be unwise to dismiss Donald Trump's Wuhan lab leak theory, *Sydney Morning Herald*, https://www.smh.com.au/national/it-would-be-unwise-to-dismiss-donald-trump-s-wuhan-lab-leak-theory-20200507-p54qyg.html.

[68] *The Lancet* published research suggesting the wet market may not have been the source of the coronavirus outbreak. See, e.g., Huang C., Wang, Y., Li, X., Ren, L., Zhao, J., Hu, Y., Zhang, L., Fan, G., Xu, J., Gu, X., Cheng, Z., Yu, T., Xia, J., Wei, Y., Wu, W., Xie, X., Yin, W., Li, H., Liu, M., ... Cao, B. (2020). Clinical features of patients infected with 2019 novel coronavirus in Wuhan, China, *Lancet*, 395(10223), 497–506, https://doi.org/10.1016/S0140-6736(20)30183-5.

[69] Butler, D. (2015, November 12). Engineered bat virus stirs debate over risky research. *Nature* News. https://www.nature.com/news/engineered-bat-virus-stirs-debate-over-risky-research-1.18787

[70] Gertz, B. (2020, May 14). Chinese deception fuels fears of ethnic biological weapons "experiments." *Washington Times.* https://m.washingtontimes.com/news/2020/may/14/china-deception-fuels-fears-biological-weapons-eth/

[71] Yuan Zhiming, director of the Wuhan Institute of Virology, categorically denied that the lab was the source of the coronavirus pandemic. Yuan cited

rigorous safety procedures and protocols. See Stanway, D., (2020, April 28), China lab rejects COVID-19 conspiracy claims, but virus origins still a mystery, *Reuters*, https://www.reuters.com/article/us-health-coronavirus-china-lab/china-lab-rejects-covid-19-conspiracy-claims-but-virus-origins-still-a-mystery-idUSKCN22A0MM. In 2018, however, a State Department team found that the Institute, a P4 biosafety lab, was not taking adequate precautions and warned that a SARS-like pandemic could result. See Rogin, J., (2020, April 14), State Department cables warned of safety issues at Wuhan lab studying bat coronaviruses, *Washington Post*, https://www.washingtonpost.com/opinions/2020/04/14/state-department-cables-warned-safety-issues-wuhan-lab-studying-bat-coronaviruses/.

[72] Lentzos, F. (2020, May 1). Natural spillover or research lab leak? Why a credible investigation is needed to determine the origin of the coronavirus pandemic. *Bulletin of the Atomic Scientists*. https://thebulletin.org/2020/05/natural-spillover-or-research-lab-leak-why-a-credible-investigation-in-needed-to-determine-the-origin-of-the-coronavirus-pandemic/#

[73] Xi Jinping, in his address to the World Health Assembly in May 2020, introduced what could be called "vaccine diplomacy." "COVID-19 vaccine development and deployment in China, when available, will be made a global public good," he promised. "This will be China's contribution to ensuring vaccine accessibility and affordability in developing countries." Watch the speech on C-SPAN: https://www.c-span.org/video/?472253-1/chinese-president-xi-world-health-assembly-address.

[74] See, e.g., Lubold, G., & Volz, D., (2020, May 14), U.S. says Chinese, Iranian hackers seek to steal coronavirus research, *Wall Street Journal*, https://www.wsj.com/articles/chinese-iranian-hacking-may-be-hampering-search-for-coronavirus-vaccine-officials-say-11589362205.

[75] Wen, W. (2020, March 30). COVID-19 blunders signal end of "American Century." *Global Times* (Beijing). https://www.globaltimes.cn/content/1184201.shtml

[76] People's Daily Online. (2020, May 18). *U.S. is to blame for global pneumonia outbreak.* http://en.people.cn/n3/2020/0518/c98649-9691334.html.

[77] See, e.g., Yi, W., (2017, September 1), *Forge ahead under the guidance of General Secretary Xi Jinping's thought on diplomacy*, Ministry of Foreign Affairs of the People's Republic of China, https://www.fmprc.gov.cn/mfa_eng/zxxx_662805/t1489143.shtml.

[78] China's unrelenting propaganda campaign against the United States, especially evident since the beginning of February, indicates that Beijing's actions in the early stages of the epidemic were to obtain geopolitical mastery. See Chang, G. G., (2020, March 12), *Gordon G. Chang: China falsely blames US for coronavirus pandemic*, Fox News,

https://www.foxnews.com/opinion/gordon-g-chang-china-falsely-blames-us-for-coronavirus-pandemic; and Chang, G. G., (2020, February 13), *Why is China blaming America for spreading 'panic' over the coronavirus?* National Interest, https://nationalinterest.org/blog/buzz/why-china-blaming-america-spreading-panic-over-coronavirus-123186.

[79] See note 18.

[80] Guarascio, F. (2020, April 8). EU urges states to lift drug export bans to prevent shortages. *Reuters.* https://www.reuters.com/article/us-health-coronavirus-eu-drug/eu-urges-states-to-lift-drug-export-bans-to-prevent-shortages-idUSKCN21Q2OT

[81] Gibson, R., & J Singh, J. P. (2018). *China Rx: Exposing the risks of America's dependence on China for medicine.* Prometheus Books, p. 195.

[82] Priest, C. (2019, July 31). *Regarding the military health system before the U.S.-China Economic and Security Review Commission* [written testimony]. U.S.-China Commission. https://www.uscc.gov/sites/default/files/Priest%20US-China%20Commission%20Statement.pdf

[83] Office of the U.S. Trade Representative. (2018, May 17). *Section 301 tariffs public hearing.* https://ustr.gov/sites/default/files/enforcement/301Investigations/Hearing%20Transcript%2C%20Proposed%20Tariffs%20Day%203.pdf

[84] Lei, W., Ting, T., Jiaying, Z. (2018, August 22). *How Zhejiang Medicine was able to avoid U.S. tariffs.* China Global Television Network. https://news.cgtn.com/news/3d3d414e33596a4e79457a6333566d54/share_p.html

[85] Reuters. (2020, April 11). Taiwan, WHO spar again over coronavirus information sharing. https://www.reuters.com/article/us-health-coronavirus-taiwan/taiwan-who-spar-again-over-coronavirus-information-sharing-idUSKCN21T0BA

[86] McNeil, D. G., Jr. (2017, May 13). Candidate to lead the W.H.O. accused of covering up epidemics. *New York Times.* https://www.nytimes.com/2017/05/13/health/candidate-who-director-general-ethiopia-cholera-outbreaks.html

[87] Buranyi, S. (2020, April 10). The WHO v coronavirus: Why it can't handle the pandemic. *The Guardian.* https://www.theguardian.com/news/2020/apr/10/world-health-organization-who-v-coronavirus-why-it-cant-handle-pandemic

[88] *The Guardian* staff and agencies. (2017, October 22). Robert Mugabe removed as WHO goodwill ambassador after outcry. *The Guardian.* https://www.theguardian.com/world/2017/oct/22/robert-mugabe-removed-as-who-goodwill-ambassador-after-outcry

[89] Cheng, M. (2017, May 22). *AP Exclusive: Strapped UN health agency spends big on travel*. Associated Press. https://apnews.com/3d8569ea7bd140e4ba02bc1712cd12ab/AP-Exclusive:-Strapped-UN-health-agency-spends-big-on-travel

[90] Associated Press. (2019, May 20). World Health Organization blew almost $192 million on travel: Report. *New York Post*. https://nypost.com/2019/05/20/world-health-organization-blew-almost-192-million-on-travel-report/

[91] Headley, T. (2018, December 2). Introducing "the poor man's atomic bomb": Biological weapons. *The National Interest*. https://nationalinterest.org/blog/buzz/introducing-poor-mans-atomic-bomb-biological-weapons-37437

[92] Bipartisan Commission on Biodefense. (2018). *A national blueprint for biodefense: Leadership and major reform needed to optimize efforts* (third printing), p. 4. https://biodefensecommission.org/wp-content/uploads/2015/10/NationalBluePrintNov2018-03.pdf

[93] Gordon, M. R. (2002, March 23). A nation challenged: Weapons; U.S. says it found Qaeda Lab being built to produce anthrax. *New York Times*. https://www.nytimes.com/2002/03/23/world/nation-challenged-weapons-us-says-it-found-qaeda-lab-being-built-produce-anthrax.html

[94] Khaniejo, N. (2016, July–December). Use of chemical and biological weapons by Daesh/ISIS. *CBW Magazine*, *9*(3), 12–16.

[95] Williams, P. (2018, March 4). MI5 horror warning: ISIS "making bio-weapons" in secret UK terror labs. *Daily Star*. https://www.dailystar.co.uk/news/latest-news/mi5-bosses-isis-jihadi-bio-18886767

[96] Soffer, A. (2013, October 16). *Experts warn of Al Qaeda biological weapons threat*. Israel National News. http://www.israelnationalnews.com/News/News.aspx/172897

[97] Ynet News. (2014, September 1). *ISIS laptop reveals project to build biological weapons*. https://www.ynetnews.com/articles/0,7340,L-4566367,00.html

[98] See note 92.

[99] Grady, D. (2019, August 5). Deadly germ research is shut down at army lab over safety concerns. *New York Times*. https://www.nytimes.com/2019/08/05/health/germs-fort-detrick-biohazard.html

[100] Kaiser, J. (2014, July 8). Six vials of smallpox discovered in U.S. lab. *Science*. https://www.sciencemag.org/news/2014/07/six-vials-smallpox-discovered-us-lab

[101] Yang, C. (2020, April 9). Documentary explores the origins of the CCP virus. *The Epoch Times.* https://www.theepochtimes.com/who-created-the-ccp-virus-documentary-exposes-pandemic-origins_3305798.html

[102] Whitehouse, S. (2015, March 12). Remarks at meeting 3 of the Blue Ribbon Study Panel on Biodefense: Surveillance and detection. Cited in Blue Ribbon Study Panel on Biodefense, (October 2015), *A national blueprint for biodefense: Leadership and major reform needed to optimize efforts,* p. 45, https://biodefensecommission.org/wp-content/uploads/2019/07/NationalBluePrintNov2018-1.pdf

[103] Vespa, M. (2020, March 18). *China lied and people died: Chinese scientists destroyed Wuhan coronavirus evidence in December.* Townhall. https://townhall.com/tipsheet/mattvespa/2020/03/18/china-destroyed-wuhan-coronavirus-evidence-n2565206

[104] Smits, M., & Weinthal, B. (2020, May 6). EU should sanction Iranian airlines exporting coronavirus and terror. *Washington Examiner,* https://www.washingtonexaminer.com/opinion/op-eds/eu-should-sanction-iranian-airlines-exporting-coronavirus-and-terror

[105] Baird, R. P. (2020, March 16). What went wrong with coronavirus testing in the U.S. *The New Yorker.* https://www.newyorker.com/news/news-desk/what-went-wrong-with-coronavirus-testing-in-the-us

[106] McCammon, S. (2020, April 5). *Hospitals reject Trump's claim they are really thrilled with supplies.* National Public Radio. https://www.npr.org/sections/coronavirus-live-updates/2020/04/05/827671323/hospitals-reject-trumps-claim-they-are-really-thrilled-with-supplies

[107] Mallapaty, S. (2020, March 6). Why does the coronavirus spread so easily between people? *Nature.* https://www.nature.com/articles/d41586-020-00660-x

[108] Groth, L. (2020, April 6). Asymptomatic carriers may still transmit coronavirus, says new research. *Health.* https://www.health.com/condition/infectious-diseases/coronavirus/asymptomatic-carriers-coronavirus

[109] Reiff, N. (2020, March 26). *The top ten biotechnology companies.* Investopedia. https://www.investopedia.com/articles/markets/122215/worlds-top-10-biotechnology-companies-jnj-rogvx.asp

[110] Phanthura, T. (2019, November 14). *Top 25 biotech companies of 2019.* Genetic Engineering and Biotechnology News. https://www.genengnews.com/a-lists/top-25-biotech-companies-of-2019/.

[111] U.S. Department of Justice. (2020, January 28). *Harvard University Professor and Two Chinese Nationals Charged in Three Separate China Related Cases* [press release]. Office of Public Affairs. https://www.justice.gov/opa/pr/harvard-

university-professor-and-two-chinese-nationals-charged-three-separate-china-related

[112] Weinberger, S.; Winter, J. and De Bourmontcorr, M. (2020, March 30). Suspected SARS virus and flu samples found in luggage: FBI report describes China's 'biosecurity risk. Yahoo News. https://news.yahoo.com/suspected-sars-virus-and-flu-found-in-luggage-fbi-report-describes-chinas-biosecurity-risk-144526820.html

[113] According to the National Cancer Institute, an enveloped virus has an outer lipid envelope. This envelope comes from the infected cell in a process called "budding off." During the budding process, newly formed virus particles become "enveloped" or wrapped in an outer coat that is made from a small piece of the cell's plasma membrane. The envelope may play a role in helping a virus survive and infect other cells. National Institute of Health website. https://www.cancer.gov/publications/dictionaries/cancer-terms/def/enveloped-virus

[114] World Health Organization (2005, October 5). *Stop the global epidemic of chronic disease* [press release]. https://www.who.int/mediacentre/news/releases/2005/pr47/en/

[115] While each of the countries may have addressed systems biology, China's title was "Systems biology further revealing population-specific genetic markers." It can be viewed in the Seventh Review Conference of the States Parties to the Convention on the Prohibition of the Development, Production and Stockpiling of Bacteriological (Biological) and Toxin Weapons and on Their Destruction, (2011, December 5–22), *Background information document submitted by the Implementation Support Unit; Addendum Annex: Submissions from States Parties* (BWC/CONF.VII/INF.3/Add.1): *Systems biology further revealing population-specific genetic markers*, Geneva, pp. 2–3, http://www.opbw.org/rev_cons/7rc/BWC_CONF.VII_INF3_Add1_E.pdf

[116] General Advisory Committee on Arms Control and Disarmament (1984, October). *A Quarter Century of Soviet Compliance Practices Under Arms Control Commitments: 1958–1983*. Unclassified summary transmitted to the Speaker of the House of Representatives, p. 2.

[117] President Reagan stated his reasons in the first such report, released in January 1983: "If the concept of arms control is to have meaning and credibility as a contribution to global or regional stability, it is essential that all parties to agreements comply with them. Because I seek genuine arms control, I am committed to ensuring that existing agreements are observed. In 1982 increasing concerns about Soviet noncompliance with arms control agreements led me to establish a senior group within the Administration to examine verification and compliance issues." The White House. (1984, January 23). *The President's report to the Congress on Soviet noncompliance with arms control agreements*. Office of the Press Secretary. https://www.cia.gov/library/readingroom/docs/CIA-RDP86B00337R000100100002-1.pdf

[118] Amendment to the Arms Control and Disarmament Act, 22 U.S.C. § 2592, Pub. L. No. 100-213, 101 Stat. 1446 (1987), Sec. 5. Compliance reports. Usually referred to as the "Pell Amendment."

[119] U.S. Arms Control and Disarmament Agency. (1992, June 24). *1990 and 1991 annual reports: Adherence to and compliance with agreements* (Sec. 52). U.S. Government Printing Office, p. 303. https://play.google.com/books/reader?id=lTg1AAAAIAAJ&hl=en&pg=GBS.PA3

[120] U.S. Arms Control and Disarmament Agency. (1993, January 14). *Adherence to and Compliance with Arms Control Agreements and the President's Report to Congress on Soviet Noncompliance with Arms Control Agreements*, Washington, DC: US Arms Control and Disarmament Agency, January 14, 1993.

[121] U.S. State Department. (2005, April 18). *Challenges of nonproliferation noncompliance*. Bureau of National Security and Nonproliferation, p. 17. https://2009-2017.state.gov/documents/organization/52113.pdf

[122] Whitby, S., Novossiolova, T., Walther, G., & Dando, M. (Eds.). (2015). *Preventing biological threats: What you can do. a guide to biological security issues and how to address them*. Bradford Disarmament Research Centre, University of Bradford, West Yorkshire, U.K., pp. 222–224.

[123] Mauroni, A. (2017, August 1). *We don't need another national biodefense strategy*, Modern War Institute at West Point. https://mwi.usma.edu/dont-need-another-national-biodefense-strategy/

[124] Melton, M. (2018, September 14). *U.S. unveils new biodefense strategy*. Voice of America. https://www.voanews.com/usa/us-unveils-new-biodefense-strategy

[125] Burns, R. (2018, September 18). *White House sets "new direction" in biodefense strategy*. Associated Press. https://apnews.com/4c21af485a7d4ccebb22f7316b55d014/White-House-sets-'new-direction'-in-biodefense-strategy

[126] Oswald, R. (2020, April 7). White House preparedness for pandemic threat has faltered across four presidencies. *Roll Call*. https://www.rollcall.com/2020/04/07/minimizing-biodefense-has-been-fault-of-four-presidents/

[127] Biesecker, M., & Krisher, T. (2020, May 11). *Becoming "king of ventilators" may result in unexpected US glut*. Associated Press. https://apnews.com/e08621567fd8758c89b0c5aed5ac5d72

[128] Holmdahl, I., & Buckee, C. (2020, May 15). Wrong but useful—What Covid-19 epidemiologic models can and cannot tell us. *New England Journal of Medicine*. https://doi.org/10.1056/NEJMp2016822

[129] See note 128.

[130] Melillo, L. (2020, January 30). *Here's how disease outbreaks can affect the economy*. WorldAtlas. worldatlas.com/articles/here-s-how-disease-outbreaks-can-affect-the-economy.html

131 Hansen, R. J. (2020, April 28). Rep. Gosar joins liberal Democrat to push Trump for biodefense changes. *Arizona Central.* https://www.azcentral.com/story/news/politics/arizona/2020/04/28/rep-paul-gosar-calls-faster-biodefense-reforms-national-biodefense-strategy/3037360001/; and Oswald, note 126.

132 Preston, R. (1998). *The Cobra Event.* Random House.

133 A detailed description of the concerns about the Soviet biological weapons program can be found in Miller, J., Engelberg, S., & Broad, W., (2001), *Germs: Biological weapons and America's secret war,* Simon and Schuster. The visits to former Soviet BW facilities and the trilateral talks are described in Kelly, D., (2002), The trilateral agreement: Lessons for biological weapons verification, in T. Findlay & O. Meier (eds.), *Verification Yearbook 2002,* (London: Verification Research, Training and Information Centre (VERTIC), 2002).

134 The Commission on the Intelligence Capabilities of the United States Regarding Weapons of Mass Destruction. (2005, March 31). *Report to the president.* Government Printing Office, p. 82.

135 There is extensive literature on assessments of Iraq's WMD programs and of inspections in Iraq. See, for example, Smithson, A. E., (2011). *Germ gambits,* Stanford University Press. A balanced and brief summary from an intelligence insider of some of the key findings related to intelligence performance is found in Petersen, M., (2017, September), Reflections on readings on 9/11, Iraq WMD, and detention and interrogation program, *Studies in Intelligence,* 61(3), 31–44.

136 Kaplan, D. E. (2000) Aum Shinrikyo, in J. B. Tucker (ed.), *Toxic terror: Assessing terrorist use of chemical and biological weapons.* MIT Press.

137 See note 132. Various sources have reported on President Clinton's reading of the book and his tasking of government agencies. See, for example, Miller et al., note 133, pp. 223–226.

138 The meeting is described in Miller et al., note 133, pp. 235–241.

139 Drell, S. D., Sofaer, A. D., & Wilson, G. D. (eds.). (1999). *The New Terror: Facing the threat of biological and chemical weapons.* The Hoover Institution Press, p. 133.

140 The conference is summarized in an extensive published volume: see note 139.

141 Winslow, F. E., (1999), The first responder's perspective, in Drell et al., note 139, p. 384. Winslow was then director, Office of Emergency Services, City of San Jose, California.

142 Nash, B. (writer), Peabody, F. (writer & director). (2001, May 7). Chemical and biological weapons (Season 8, Episode 13) [TV series episode]. In D. Cambou &

B. Dietrich (Executive Producers), *Modern Marvels*, Al Roker Productions, American Dad.

[143] Gannon, J. C., (2000, January), The global infectious disease threat and its implications for the United States (NIE 99-17D), National Intelligence Council. John Gannon describes the origin and reaction to the estimate and the subsequent Global Trends series in his chapter A new global agenda: 1997–2001, (2019), in R. Hutchings & G. F. Treverton (eds.), *Truth to power: A history of the U.S. National Intelligence Council* (pp. 57–84), Oxford University Press.

[144] The phrase *the sum of all fears* came into popular province with the 1991 book by Tom Clancy and later movie with the same name. The origin, though, appears to be a quote from Winston Churchill, November 16, 1943: "Why, you may take the most gallant sailor, the most intrepid airman or the most audacious soldier, put them at a table together—what do you get? The sum of their fears."

[145] Defense Science Board, (2007, May), *Defense Science Board 2005 summer study on reducing vulnerabilities to weapons of mass destruction*, Office of the Under Secretary of Defense. There were other, similar contemporary studies, such as those conducted by the Advisory Panel to Assess Domestic Response Capabilities for Terrorism Involving Weapons of Mass Destruction (better known as the Gilmore Commission).

[146] See note 145, pp. xii–xiii.

INDEX

1984 Arms Control and
Disarmament Act, 123
2019-nCoV coronavirus, 19, 20
9/11 Commission, 2
9/11 terrorist attacks, 61
Abrini, Muhammed, 63
Adaptive immunity, 104
Afghanistan, 63, 122
al Qaeda, 63
Alibek, Ken, 6, 83, 99, 154
anthrax, 5, 37, 39, 63, 64, 65, 74,
75, 85, 101, 140, 141, 142, 145
anthroponosis, 94
anthropozoonosis, 24, 75, 80, 94
Arms Control and Disarmament
Act, 123
Arrow III, 81
Aum Shinrikyo, 138, 140
Australia, 34, 37, 54, 55, 107, 118
Aylward, Bruce, 52, 53, 57
Azithromycin, 37
bats, 4, 9, 12, 13, 14, 17, 19, 20,
21, 22, 24, 75
Belgium, 38
bin Laden, Osama, 63, 141
Biological Weapons Convention,
6, 32, 62, 74, 88, 116, 120, 121,
123, 124, 126, 133, 152
Bioterrorism Risk Assessment,
100
Biowarfare, 36, 38
Bipartisan Commission on
Biodefense, 1, 2, 30, 62, 64, 66,
80, 126, 130, 131
Birx, Deborah, 31
Boston Children's Hospital, 17
Botao Xiao, 17, 19, 20
botulinum, 140, 141
Bristol Myers Squibb, 40
Bryen, Shoshana, 5, 73

Bryen, Stephen, 5, 73
Bush, George W., 148
Canada, 37, 76, 107
Cell Research, 13
Chan, Margaret, 57, 58
Chang, Gordon, 4, 5, 23, 49, 65
Chen Qiushi, 27
Chen Quanjiao, 17
Chen Wei, 32
chimeric coronaviruses, 32
China Global Television Network,
17
China Rx, 5, 38, 153
China's Great Firewall, 52
Chinese Academy of Military
Medical Sciences Institute of
Microbiology and
Epidemiology, 75
Chinese Center for Disease
Control and Prevention
(Beijing), 25
Chinese Institute of Virology, 20
Chinese Ministry of Commerce,
41
Chinese Ministry of Science and
Technology, 25
Chinese National Health
Commission, 27, 28, 30
Chinese National University of
Defense Technology, 32
chloroquine, 13, 102
CIA, 5, 7, 29, 63, 79, 151, 152
Ciprofloxacin, 37
Civica Rx, 44
Clinton, Bill, 141, 142, 148
Cooperative Threat Reduction
Program, 142
Coronavirus Taskforce, 131
Cotton, Tom, 3
CoV ZC45, 19

COVID-19, 1, 6, 13, 16, 17, 22, 23, 24, 25, 26, 27, 29, 31, 33, 51, 52, 53, 54, 57, 65, 66, 69, 70, 75, 76, 86, 90, 92, 94, 95, 96, 97, 99, 102, 106, 107, 109, 110, 112, 115, 126, 127, 130, 131, 133, 134, 135, 136, 137, 138, 146, 147, 149
Coxsackievirus, 103
CRISPR, 75
Cui Tiankai, 23, 34
Cuomo Andrew, 131
cytokines, 108
Czech Republic, 37, 38, 118, 119
Danzig,Richard, 143
Defense Health Agency, 40
Defense Threat Reduction Agency, 142
Department of Defense, 43
Department of Health and Human Services, 43, 131
Department of Homeland Security, 33
Department of Veterans Affairs, 43
Der Spiegel, 29
DeSutter, Paula, 6, 115, 152
diphtheria, 106
Drell,Sidney, 143
Ebola, 9, 21, 22, 57, 58, 74, 85, 126
Ekeus,Rolf, 143
Elliott, Stephen, 6, 7, 129, 152
EU Commission, 45
European Medicines Agency, 37
European Union, 38, 126
Faddis, Charles, 5, 6, 61
Fauci, Anthony, 31
Federal Bureau of Investigation, 33, 75, 76, 79
Federal Emergency Management Agency, 43
fentanyl, 75

Food and Drug Administration, 37, 39, 42, 43
Ford, Gerald, 116
Fort Detrick, 6, 64
France, 16, 17, 34, 37, 38, 92
French and Indian War, 73
Gannon,John, 144
Geneva Protocol for the Prohibition of the Use in War of Asphyxiating, Poisonous or Other Gases, and of Bacteriological Methods of Warfare (1925), 116, 120, 122, 127
genome sequencing, 13, 119
Geraghty, Jim, 4, 9, 65, 153
Germany, 29, 54, 86, 118, 119
Gibson, Rosemary, 5, 35, 153
Gingrich, Newt, 141, 142, 143
Ginsburg, Ruth, 41
glanders, 85
Gorbachev, Mikhail, 85, 139
Greece, 73
Grunow-Finke Assessment Tool, 99, 100
Guam, 81
Guangdong, 12, 27, 49
Hart-Rudman Commission, 2
Harvard Center for Communicable Disease Dynamics, 132
Harvard Medical School, 17, 27
hemorrhagic fever, 101
History Channel, 144
HK01, 17
Hong Kong, 16, 17, 30, 34, 52, 53, 57
Hoover Institution, 143
Huanan Seafood Wholesale Market, 25
Huang Yanling, 14, 16, 17
Hubei, 3, 16, 19, 21, 23, 25, 29, 31, 37, 91

human-to-human transmissibility, 4, 27, 28, 29, 48, 69, 76
Hussein, Saddam, 73, 86, 138, 140
Imam Hossein University, 74
India, 38, 40, 78
Innate immunity, 104
interferon, 109
interferons, 105
interleukins, 108
International Civil Aviation Organization, 57
International Telecommunication Union, 56
Intourist, 52
Iran, 53, 62, 67, 68, 74, 86
ISIS, 62, 63
Israel, 73, 78, 81, 152
Ivins, Bruce, 64
Japan, 44, 49, 73, 81
Jewish Policy Center, 5
JQKNews.com, 21
Kazakhstan, 34, 39, 142
Kenya, 141
Khobar Towers terrorist attack, 141
Kuwait, 138
Lanzhou Institute of Biological Products, 75
Lauder, John, 7, 137, 153, 154
Lederberg, John, 141, 150
Lei Xiao, 19
Li Qun, 28
Li Wenliang, 26, 76
Lieberman, Joe, 2
Lugar,Richard, 142
Lyme disease, 103
Malek Ashtar University, 74
Manchuria, 84
Marburg hemorrhagic fever, 85
Mayo Clinic, 44
medetomidine, 75
melioidosis, 85

MI5, 63
Middlebury Institute of International Studies at Monterey, 75
Military World Games, 2019, 51
Moltke the Elder, 136
Monath, Tom, 142
Mugabe Robert, 58
Muhammed Abrini, 63
Murrah Federal Building, 141
Mycotoxins, 73
N-95 masks, 36, 81
National Biodefense Strategy, 2018, 2, 6, 129, 134, 135, 136
National Defense Authorization Act, 2017, 2, 129, 136
National Institutes of Health, 22, 65, 79
National Intelligence Council, 144
National Review, 4, 9, 153
National Security Advisor, 131
National Security Council, 131, 151
Netherlands, 37, 106, 119
New England Journal of Medicine, 132
New York, 131
Nixon, Richard, 73, 85
North Korea, 53, 62, 74, 75, 86
Nunn,Sam, 142
Oak Ridge National Laboratory, 38
Okinawa, 81
Osnos, Evan, 32
Pangolins, 13
Peking University, 28
Pell Report, 123
Pell, Claiborne, 123
Peng Liyuan, 57
Penicillin Cartel, 40
pertussis, 106
Piperacillin/tazobactam, 37
plague, 49, 63, 64, 75, 84, 85, 101
Plague of Athens, 73

pneumonia, 12, 41, 47, 53
Poland, 38, 118, 119
Pompeo, Mike, 54
Portugal, 119
President's Foreign Intelligence
  Advisory Panel, 143
Priest, Christopher, 40, 163
Public Health Emergency of
  International Concern
  (PHEIC), 49
Q-fever, 85
Radio France Internationale, 16,
  17
remdesivir, 13
Rhinolophus affinis, 19
Rice,Condoleezza, 143
ricin, 63
Ridge, Thomas, 2, 130
Robb-Silberman Commission, 2,
  140
Rogers, Mike, 62
Rosett, Claudia, 5, 47, 154
Russia, 62, 65, 74, 76, 77, 142,
  148
Russian State Center of Virology
  and Biotechnology (VECTOR),
  65, 74, 142
SARS, 9, 12, 13, 20, 21, 22, 29, 31,
  32, 51, 52, 53, 57, 76, 90, 91,
  93, 94, 96, 97, 98, 102, 106,
  126, 151
Scientific American, 12
Shanghai Media Group, 21
Shanghai Public Health Clinical
  Center, 30
Sherman Act, 41
Shi Zhengli, 12, 14
Shultz,George, 143
smallpox, 5, 6, 65, 73, 74, 75, 84,
  85, 86, 87, 88, 89, 90, 92, 93,
  94, 95, 96, 97, 98, 101, 107,
  142
Solovetsky Islands, 85
South Africa, 86, 118

South China Morning Post, 16, 30
South China University of
  Technology, 17
South Korea, 49
Soviet Union, 6, 66, 85, 86, 88,
  121, 122, 123, 124, 137, 138,
  139, 148, 151, 154
Spanish Flu, 135
Spanish Flu pandemic, 99
Stanford University, 143
Staphylococcal enterotoxin B, 85
Stepnogorsk, 142
Sweden, 119
Syria, 62, 63, 147
Taiwan, 34, 52, 53, 54, 57, 78, 80,
  81
Taiwan Centers for Disease
  Control, 53
Talent-Graham Commission, 2
Tanzania, 141
Tedros Adhanom Ghebreyesus, 5,
  25, 29, 47, 49, 50, 54, 55, 57,
  58
Tenet, George, 63
tetanus, 106
Thailand, 49, 92
The Cobra Event, 138, 141, 148
Thucydides, 73
Tian Junhua, 20, 21
Tian You Hospital, 19
tianxia, 33
Tokyo, 138, 140
Transbaikalia, 84
Trump, Donald, 2, 3, 6, 7, 25, 43,
  49, 50, 54, 55, 56, 59, 67, 129,
  132, 151
  China travel ban, 3, 35
Tsai Ing-wen, 54
Tskhay, Albina, 6, 83, 99
tuberculosis, 58, 106, 107
tularemia, 85, 101
Tye, Matthew, 9, 12, 14, 16, 17

U.S. Army Medical Research Institute of Infectious Diseases (USAMRIID), 64
U.S. bioweapons program, 74
U.S. Centers for Disease Control and Prevention, 16, 19, 25
U.S. Department of State, 62
U.S. Navy, 77, 81
U.S. Supreme Court, 41
U.S. Trade Representative, 40
UN Food and Agriculture Organization, 25, 56
UN Industrial Development Organization, 57
UNESCO, 59
United Kingdom, 36, 37, 54, 86, 118, 119, 135, 139
USS *Ronald Reagan*, 78
USS *Theodore Roosevelt*, 77
Valisure, 42
valsartan, 42
Venezuelan equine encephalomyelitis, 85
Venter, Craig, 141
Ventilators, 37, 67
Vietnam, 78
Wall Street Journal, 20, 28, 154
Walter Reed Army Institute of Research, 25
Wang Guangfa, 28
Wang Huning, 27
Wang Mengyue, 14, 16
Wang Yi, 33
Wei Cuihua, 14, 16
Weibo, 17
wet market, 24, 25, 26
Whitehouse, Sheldon, 66

World Health Assembly, 24, 54, 55, 56
World Health Organization, 1, 2, 5, 12, 13, 19, 20, 24, 25, 28, 29, 30, 47, 48, 49, 50, 51, 52, 53, 54, 55, 56, 57, 58, 59, 65, 76, 80, 110, 126, 133
World Trade Center, 61
Wuhan, 3, 4, 12, 13, 14, 17, 19, 20, 22, 23, 24, 25, 26, 27, 28, 29, 30, 31, 32, 33, 37, 47, 48, 49, 50, 51, 52, 53, 54, 65, 70, 75, 76, 91
Wuhan Center for Disease Control and Prevention, 19, 20, 22
Wuhan Institute of Virology, 9, 12, 13, 14, 17, 20, 22, 24, 30, 32, 52
Wuhan University of Science and Technology, 19
Xi Jinping, 24, 25, 27, 28, 29, 33, 49, 50, 54, 56, 57
Xi, Jinping, 31, 33, 34, 47, 49
Xiaobo Tao, 17
Xiaobo, Tao, 17
Xiaoxu Sean Lin, 25
Xinhua News Agency, 21
Yousef, Ramzi, 141
Yunnan Province, 12, 13, 19
Zhao Lijian, 33, 51
Zhejiang Hisun Pharmaceutical Company, 39
Zhejiang Novus Pharmaceuticals, 40
Zhejiang province, 19
Zhen Shuji, 16
Zhong Nanshan, 27, 28

Made in the USA
Las Vegas, NV
22 November 2024

12416165R00105